CW00969030

•Bartholom

WALKING IN
BRITTANY

by Brian Spencer

Bartholomew
An Imprint of HarperCollins*Publishers*

CONTENTS

A Bartholomew Walk Guide
Published by Bartholomew
An Imprint of HarperCollins*Publishers*
77-85 Fulham Palace Road
London W6 8JB

First published 1995
© Bartholomew 1995

Printed in Hong Kong

ISBN 0 7028 2798 3
95/1/15

LOCATION MAP

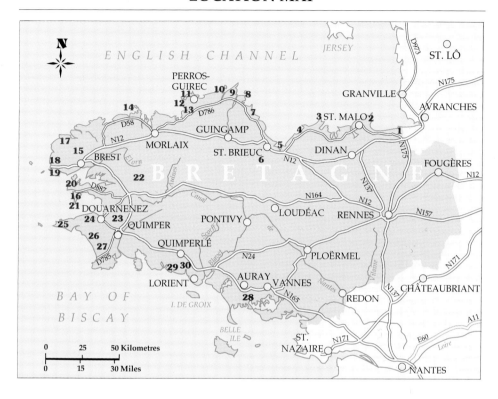

KEY TO ROUTE MAPS

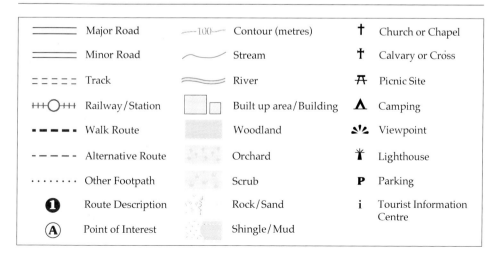

═══	Major Road	⋯100⋯	Contour (metres)	✝	Church or Chapel
══	Minor Road	∿	Stream	✝	Calvary or Cross
= = = =	Track	≈≈	River	⊼	Picnic Site
┼┼◯┼┼	Railway/Station	▢ ▫	Built up area/Building	▲	Camping
▪ ▪ ▪ ▪	Walk Route		Woodland	☀	Viewpoint
─ ─ ─	Alternative Route		Orchard	✲	Lighthouse
⋯⋯⋯	Other Footpath		Scrub	P	Parking
❶	Route Description		Rock/Sand	i	Tourist Information Centre
Ⓐ	Point of Interest		Shingle/Mud		

BRITTANY, THE MAGICAL LAND

Golden sandy beaches, rocky coves and dramatic headlands, timeless stone villages, lush fields and silent forests, make this maritime corner of France an idyllic haven.

Most visitors go to Brittany for its sea, sunshine and beaches. Its popularity as a holiday region began with the development of mass transport during the Edwardian era, and the hotels and resorts that came with it fill large sections of the coastline. Busy and populous it may be, yet Brittany still has mile upon mile of untrodden beaches, airy cliff tops and colourful, yet enigmatic, moorlands. Anyone who seeks out-of-the-way places, will find them here.

Brittany has long attracted the British to its shores; its very name means 'Little Britain', a title first given to it by the Celts who lived on the far western peninsulas of Europe's outer-most lands. Harried by a long history of invasions which began with colonising Romans, closely followed by rampaging Saxons and Vikings, the people of Brittany have great similarities with Welsh, Irish and Cornish folk. The ancient language of the Bretons has many words which are common to each race and many of their legends have crossed national boundaries.

A land of enigmas, the first people to inhabit Brittany, in Neolithic times, built huge stone structures, megaliths, dolmens and the like. Why they built them and for what purpose is unknown, but the stones have posed those unanswered questions down the centuries. We are no closer to the truth than the men and women who later created legends around those enigmas. Once a source of great power, many of them were converted to Christian symbols and even now are the centrepoint of religious festivals.

Throughout the ages, myths and supernatural beliefs have grown around the megalithic remains. In view of the size of so many of the stones, it is not surprising that stories of giants have grown around them. Giants like Hok-Bras and Gargantua are credited with erecting many of the stones. Hok-Bras was a gentle giant who had a fairy godmother. She lived in a dense part of the Huelgoat Forest and gave him the power to stretch as far as he liked. One day, wishing to get a glimpse of her, he simply piled rocks on top of each other, making what became known as the Monts d'Arrée. Gargantua was an entirely different sort of giant. Whenever the locals refused to feed him, or gave him something he didn't like, he threw huge rocks at them, and once swallowed a fishing boat whole. Born on the moors near Cap Fréhel, there are still traces of him dotted about the countryside. His finger is now the standing stone near Fort Lalatte and a boulder near the village of Chablé is one of his teeth!

Fairies live in some of the ancient mounds and dance around the standing stones at midnight at certain times of the year. A huge passage grave made of 41 stone blocks near Essé, called the *Roche aux Fées* (the fairy rock), is said to be one of their palaces. *Korrigans* (elves) live on the windswept moors or deep inside the silent forests. Guardians of the stones, they also assist the fairies with their work. A happy race, they will help any human who is kind to them, but woe betide anyone who does anything to annoy them.

In a land of fairies and giants, wicked witches also have their part to play in Breton legends. One of them, called Gwrac'h, specialised in changing her husbands into fish, which she then fried in a pan made from gold. *Morganezed* (mermaids) and *morganed* (mermen) live beneath the waves of this storm-lashed coast, luring unfortunate sailors to their deaths. Most of them live in the sea off the Île d'Ouessant (Ushant Island), a region of fog banks and a merciless ocean. Shy beautiful creatures, with blue eyes and long blond hair, they occasionally come ashore to dry their treasures.

Legends of King Arthur link Brittany with south-west England; in fact the south-west corner of Finistère is known as *Cornouaille*, or Cornwall. The Brocéliande Forest near Paimpont is also known as Merlin's Forest and is where Lancelot, who loved Guinevere, King Arthur's wife, was born.

Towns and villages swallowed by the sea's encroachment of the land have remained in folk memory as mythical cities. The city of Ys is supposed to be beneath the waves in the Baie de

Douarnenez. It was built on reclaimed *polder-land* and was protected by a seawall with a door which only the king could open. His name was Gradlon and he had a beautiful daughter called Dahud. The Devil was attracted to Dahud and disguised himself as a handsome young man in order to win her affections. He so won her over that he was able to make her steal the key to the door in the seawall. During an especially high tide, the Devil opened the sea door, flooding the city and also drowning Dahud.

BRITTANY'S FOUR DISTRICTS

Brittany is divided into four *départements*, administrative districts. **Finistère** is the most westerly département. Surrounded by the sea on three sides, cliff-lined headlands jut far out into the Atlantic. Secluded rocky coves, sail-dappled bays and dune-backed sheltered beaches, contrast with medieval towns, flower-filled rolling meadows and dark green forests. Similar in many ways to Cornwall, the ancient Breton language is still spoken here. Finistère has a number of *enclos paroissiaux* (parish closes) and groups of ecclesiastical buildings, where the church is entered through a gateway decorated with brightly-painted statues of local saints and elaborate altar pieces.

Côtes d'Armor département has a 220-mile-long coastline of sandy bays which look out on to an azure sea littered with thousands of tiny rocky islands. From Perros-Guirec to Tréburden, the sea has worn the pink and coppery granite rocks into a maze of strangely contorted shapes, giving the coast the title of the 'Pink Granite Coast'. Remote cliffs, gentler coastal dunes, inland forests and valleys dotted with tiny chapels and remote megaliths are perfect places to enjoy easy walking.

Mont St Michel, though strictly part of Normandy, is offshore from **Ille-et-Vilaine**. The département's seashore, the Emerald Coast, stretches from Mont St Michel in the east, to Dinard in the west. Protected from the prevailing winds, it has a near-Mediterranean climate, and many sub-tropical shrubs flower in parks and gardens. Land reclaimed from the sea, *polderland*, grows early crops and luxury vegetables such as artichokes and asparagus. Castle-like châteaux and half-timbered medieval towns are a link with another age.

Morbihan, the most southerly département, is where thatch-roofed, half-timbered farmhouses and stone-built cottages fit snugly into a landscape which has remained basically unchanged since the Middle Ages. A long coastline of low cliffs and sandy coves, the district takes its name from a landlocked sea, the Gulf of Morbihan. Rich in wildlife and enjoying a well above-average amount of sunshine, many rare and almost sub-tropical wild flowers bloom in sheltered recesses along its coast. Morbihan has the highest concentration of megaliths and Stone Age monuments in the world, culminating with the marching rows of aligned stones of Carnac.

THE BRETONS

The sea plays an important part in the everyday life of Breton folk. Great mariners, whose ancestors are reputed to have discovered America long before Columbus, Brittany trawlers still fish off the Labrador coast and in the cold waters around Iceland. Their hard-won catches appear on menus in Brittany restaurants, along with shellfish, crabs and lobsters from the waters around the coast. Inland, the countryside is verdant and favoured by the mild climate, and early-grown Brittany vegetables find ready markets across the Channel in Britain.

Pardons, part secular, part religious festivals, are regular events held throughout the year. Often with roots going back to pagan times, *pardons* are an excuse for Breton people to dress in their traditional costume. Varying slightly from place to place, women's costumes are usually based on dresses of elaborately patterned heavy brocade, protected by delicate lace-edged aprons. On their heads they wear the traditional starched lace stovepipe *coiffes*. Male dress is just as elaborate. The men wear black trousers, frequently the baggy *bragoubras*, and short black wide-lapelled jackets and wide, floppy black, usually be-ribboned, felt berets. Dancing is an important part of many of these festivals, when the music might still be made by the *bombarde*, a kind of oboe, and the Breton bagpipes, the *biniou*.

FRUITS OF THE SEA

Along the coast, harbours shelter a bewildering range of sea-going craft, from luxury yachts to tiny inshore fishing boats. Marinas lined with hawser rattling masts have overtaken the ancient fishing port atmosphere of the larger towns, but the quieter places are unchanged and every little creek seems to be home base for a handful of small craft. Crab fishermen are out at first light, trying their luck in the deep water surrounding the outer rocks and headlands. They set out as the deep sea fishermen return, hopefully laden with Icelandic cod, or sole from the sea bottom somewhere out in the Bay of Biscay. Many fishermen are happy to sell at least part of their catch directly from the harbour wall, the best way to buy really fresh fish.

At low tide, strange fence-like structures can be seen far out on the sandy bays, or along muddy estuaries. Known as *bouchots*, they are lines of poles sunk deep into the sand, on which grow all manner of shellfish. Tended by 'fishermen' who use amphibious tractors rather than boats, the mussels, together with cockles, oysters and scallops grown in special enclosures, find a ready market, not only locally, but in restaurants throughout the rest of Europe.

BRITTANY CUISINE

Eating well is an important part of any holiday, especially in France. Breton cookery is as varied as the region and is based on age-old recipes. Fish is an important part of Brittany menus; locally harvested *moules* (mussels), *huîtres* (oysters), and *langoustines* (crayfish), form the basis for the popular *fruits de mer*. Served on a kind of cake-stand and topped by a crab or a lobster, the seaweed decorated meal is not for anyone in a hurry. *Homard à l'Armoricaine*, lobster in a rich cream-based sauce of tomatoes, onions and brandy, is one of Brittany's prized dishes. The Bretons have their own form of *bouillabaise* (fish stew). Called *cotriade*, it is usually made from conger eel, although more or less any locally-caught fish may be used. Served with grated cheese and croutons, it is a meal in itself.

Of all the meat dishes on offer, without doubt the finest is *pré-salé*, lamb or mutton, from sheep reared on the saltmarshes around the bay of Mont St Michel. Accompanying vegetables are always fresh, grown in a region famous for its early maturing crops.

Wines are mostly from the Loire: Muscadet, Gros Plant and Anjou rosés; although cider from local orchards is the favoured drink of the true Breton.

Crêpes are probably the one dish most visitors consider synonymous with Brittany. The thin pancakes can be eaten either as a savoury rolled with ham, cheese, mushrooms or seafood, or more commonly, with jam and sugar, or flambé with a sweet liqueur. BON APPÉTIT!

LANGUAGE

The Breton language has many similarities to Welsh, and the following short list will help you understand place names more fully.

aber – estuary
bihan – small
braz – large
goat – wood (also spelt *coat*, *goët*, or *hoët*)
haras – stud farm
hir – long
ker – village
lan or *lann* – consecrated ground (usually the site of a church)
ménez – rounded hill
men – stone
mor – sea
pleu – parish (also spelt *ploë*, *plou* or *plé*, and usually followed by a saint's name)
ty – house

EVENTS AND FESTIVALS

There are times when a visitor to Brittany might be forgiven for thinking the Bretons spend all their time enjoying themselves! Almost every town and village has some kind of festival, whether it is a religious *pardon* in honour of its patron saint, an excuse to show off their local skills, or simply to enjoy themselves. Practised in many forms, festivals have become an important part of Breton culture.

Dancing is another widely followed form of entertainment. *Fest-noz*, or 'night feast', originated as a celebration marking the end of a communal activity such as harvesting. Barns and threshing floors were taken over, trestle-tables loaded with food and wine, and to the music provided by *binious* (Breton bagpipes) everyone settled down for a night of energetic dancing. Using earth-floored threshing sheds meant the ground was probably uneven and this led to the development of heavy-footed dances such as *gavottes*, or round or chain-dances, in order to pound down the earth for gentler rhythms later. Nowadays, *fest-noz* takes place in marquees or village halls, but the end result is still the same, with locals and visitors enjoying themselves to the full.

The following list is only a selection of the

activities taking place throughout the year. To find out more check with the Tourist Office nearest to your holiday centre.

Pardons
Tréguier: The Pardon of St Yves (Pardon des Pauvres). Third Sunday in May.
St Jean-du-Doigt: The Pardon of St Jean. Sunday closest 24 June.
Ste Anne-d'Auray: The Pardon of St Anne. Last weekend in July.
Dinard: The Pardon of the Sea. Third Sunday in August.
Ste Anne-la-Palud: The Pardon of Ste Anne. Last Sunday in August.
St Fiacre: The Pardon of St Fiacre. Last Sunday in August.
Le Folgoët: The Pardon of the Woodland Fool. First Sunday in September.
Carnac: The Pardon of St Cornély. Second Sunday in September.
Josselin: The Baker's Pardon. Second Sunday in September.

Festivals
St Malo: Rock Music Festival at the end of February. Festival of Jazz during the first weekend in August.
Douarnenez: Maritime festival, Port-Rhu. Pentecost weekend, around mid-May.
Rennes: les Tombées de la Nuit – Création Breton (concerts and floodlit tableaux). End of June and the beginning of July.
Nantes: Carnival and Arts Festival. Early July.
Gourin: Grande Fête de la Crêpe. Middle weekend in July.
Pont l'Abbé: Festival of Embroidery. Second Sunday in July.
Lamballe: Festival of Ajonc d'Or (the Golden Gorse), a folk festival. Second Sunday in July.
Paimpol: Festival of Newfoundland and Iceland. Third Sunday in July.
Fouesnant: Apple Festival. Third Sunday in July.
Dinan: International Music Festival. End of July.
Quimper: Cornouaille Festival (Breton culture). During the week preceding the fourth Sunday in July.
Lannion: Music Festival. July and August.
Redon: Festival of the Abbey (theatre, music and dance). From mid-July to mid-August.
Morlaix: Les Mercredis de Morlaix. Fairs and festivals. On Wednesdays in July and August.

Pont Aven: Ajonc d'Or (the Golden Gorse), Folk Festival. First Sunday in August.
Lorient: Celtic Festival. First fortnight in August.
Plomodiern/Ménez-Hom: Folklore Festival held in the village and on the nearby mountain. 15 August.
Châteauneuf-du-Faou: International Festival of Folk Dancing. 15 August.
Guingcamp: Festival of Breton music and dance. Second Sunday in August.
Cap Sizun: Heather Festival. Second Sunday in August.
St Briac: Fêtes des Mouttes (Seagull Festival); Breton dance and bands. Second Sunday in August.
Concarneau: Festival of Blue Nets. Third Sunday in August.
Carnac: Festival of the Menhirs. Third Sunday in August.
Fougères: Festival of Livre Vivant (historical pageant with *son et lumière*). End of August/beginning of September.

HOW TO GET THERE

Brittany Ferries sail direct to the heart of Brittany from ports along the south coast of England. St Malo and Roscoff are small towns, but are served with an excellent system of roads feeding into the French autoroute network. On the overnight crossings you will arrive in Brittany before mid-morning, ready for a full day's travel.

CROSSINGS – Timings vary according to tides. Check with Brittany Ferries when making reservations:

Portsmouth – St Malo. Night crossing: average time 9 hours.
St Malo – Portsmouth. Day crossing: average time 9 hours.
Poole – St Malo. Day crossing: average time 8 hours.
St Malo – Poole. Night crossing: average time 8 hours.
Plymouth – Roscoff. Night or day crossings: average time 6 hours.
Roscoff – Plymouth. Night or day crossings: average time 6 hours.

There is a choice of accommodation on night crossings, ranging from de-luxe twin-bedded suites, to two and four-berth cabins, or recliner seats. French cuisine is on offer in the highly-acclaimed restaurants or self-service cafeterias. There are lounges and bars on board, and entertainment ranges from cinemas showing current films, to dancing to the resident band. Young children have a supervised play area. All vessels have a large Duty Free shopping area.

Booking and timetable details can be obtained from your local travel agent, or direct from:

Brittany Ferries
The Brittany Centre
Wharf Road
Portsmouth PO2 8RU
Tel: (01705) 827701 – Ferry Reservations
(01705) 751833 – Inclusive Holiday Reservations

Brittany Ferries
Millbay
Plymouth PL1 3EW
Tel: (01752) 221321 – Ferry Reservations
(01752) 263388 – Inclusive Holiday Reservations
Open: Monday to Friday 0800-2000.
Saturday and Sunday 0900-1730.

In addition, Brittany Ferries operate services from Cork to Roscoff, Cork to St Malo, Portsmouth to Caen and Poole to Cherbourg. Sealink have a Weymouth to Cherbourg service, and both Sealink and P&O operate between Portsmouth and Cherbourg.

Anyone using Channel crossings into northern France and the Pas de Calais should follow the autoroutes to Paris, heading south-west from there on the A11. This road splits at Le Mans, the A11 continuing south-west to Nantes for southern Brittany, and the A81/N157 travelling west to Rennes for central and northern Brittany.

TRAVEL IN BRITTANY

Motor Insurance

Green Card Certificates are no longer required for motoring in France and other member states of the EC. However, you must have an up-to-date Insurance Policy and have advised your insurer about your plans. Your broker/agent will need to know your proposed travel dates and all the countries you intend visiting. Failure to notify your insurer would result in your policy being restricted to the minimum requirements needed to comply with the laws relating to compulsory insurance of motor vehicles in any member country of the European Community in which the vehicle is being used.

Even though travel documents are no longer examined on entry to member countries of the EC, it is advisable to carry your motor insurance certificate and the vehicle log book. Your insurance company will advise you about what action to take in the event of an accident.

Provisional licence holders are not allowed to drive in France, and the minimum age for drivers is 18.

Motoring organisations also provide extra insurance, covering personal accident and medical costs, holiday cancellation, loss of personal property, as well as vehicle breakdown, accident and theft. Their insurance schemes cover the cost of replacement vehicles, or returning home, either for yourself and passengers, or for the vehicle, should the need arise for it to travel separately. Most foreign travel insurance cover includes Letters of Credit which are repayable on return to the UK.

Driving in France

Motoring in France, despite the need to concentrate on driving on the 'wrong' side of the road, is usually more pleasurable than at home. If you are travelling away from the larger towns and outside the main holiday periods, roads are comparatively traffic free.

However, there are a few simple rules which must be observed when driving in France:

1. Have all your motoring documents available at all times.

2. Carry a spare set of light bulbs, including indicator bulbs. Failure to have a spare bulb could result in an on-the-spot fine in the event of any bulb not working.

3. Carry a red warning triangle, and in the event of a breakdown or accident, erect it 30 metres (33yds) behind your car, in clear view, without obstructing oncoming traffic.

4. Wearing seat belts is compulsory for front seat passengers. Children below the age of 10 are not allowed to travel in the front seats.

5. 'GB' stickers must be as close as possible to the rear number plate.

6. Drink/driving laws are strictly interpreted and could result in a prison sentence and the confiscation of your car. Random drink/driving checks operate and the very best you could expect to get away with, if caught, is a fine in the region of Fr2,000 to Fr 30,000.

7. In some built-up areas the *priorité à droit* rule applies and will be signposted. In this case give way to vehicles joining your road from the

right. However, this rule no longer applies at roundabouts and you must give way to cars already on the roundabout and approaching from your left. The sign you will see on approaching the roundabout is *Vous n'avez pas la priorité. Cédez la passage* means 'Give way'.

8. Speed limits (see also below), if broken, can earn an on-the-spot fine. Speeding fines are in the order of Fr300 to Fr5,000. Speed limits in built-up areas begin as soon as the name plate of a town, or village, is passed, regardless of whether a speed limit sign is shown. *Rappel* means 'slow down' and is often prior warning of a lower speed limit, say when approaching a bend, or other road hazard.

Speed Limits

Autoroutes – (A) roads – 130kph (81mph) in dry weather; and 110kph (68mph) in wet weather or poor visibility.

National Routes – (N) roads – 110kph (68mph) in dry weather; and 90kph (56mph) in wet weather or poor visibility.

Other roads – (D) roads – outside built-up areas 90kph (56mph) in dry weather; and 80kph (50mph) in wet weather or poor visibility.

Towns – 50/60kph (31mph/37mph). The speed limit varies, dependent on the road width etc.

An English language update on motorway conditions is available from Autoroute Information on: (00 33) 1 47 05 90 01. Traffic information by radio is broadcast on 89.2 or 107.7 FM.

Parking

Despite what might seem the contrary, there are rules governing parking in French towns. By-laws vary from place to place and, in market towns, from day to day. Parking in some streets is on one side on odd dates, and the other side on even dates. Many places have parking meter (*horodateur*) systems but they are usually only for a short duration; other towns have parking discs which you can obtain from the tourist office. Some car parks have a barrier which opens when a paid-up or stamped ticket is fed into a slot.

Preparing the car before driving in France

1. Buy spare bulbs and a spare fan belt, and possibly spare accelerator and clutch cables.
2. Make sure the car has been recently serviced.
3. Check the brakes and the condition of the tyres – tyre wear rules are similar to those in the UK. Check fluid levels in the brake and clutch reservoirs and make sure the battery acid level covers each cell.
4. Make sure all tyre pressures are correct (including the spare), especially if the car is going to be fully loaded with passengers and luggage.
5. An important thing to check is the antifreeze level in the car radiator. This is not as strange a tip as it may seem. Antifreeze raises the boiling point of water and hopefully the weather will be warmer in France than at home. Cooling system failure is an all too common cause of holiday breakdowns, so check the hoses and make sure they have not become soggy, or that any clips need replacing.
6. As well as the spare fan belt and cables, carry a few odds and ends that might be useful in an emergency; such as insulating tape, jump leads, a tow rope, a fire extinguisher and a can of spare fuel. (Carrying spare fuel in a can is legal in France.) Make sure you have enough tools to carry out small repairs such as tightening cables, or nuts and screws, and especially make sure that the jack will lift the car and that the wheel-securing nuts are not too tight.
7. Finally, always carry a first aid kit and learn how to use it. It might help to save lives in an emergency.

To hire a car: toll-free numbers in France
Citer: 05 05 10 11
Avis: 05 05 22 11
Hertz: 05 05 33 11
Euro Rent: 05 33 22 10
Eurocar: 05 10 05 05

Health for travellers

EEC rules allow British travellers to enjoy the same health care as French citizens. Before leaving Britain, you should obtain a Form E111 from the Post Office (this is available to anyone with a National Health registration number). The Department of Health booklet, 'Health Advice For Travellers', explains how to go about obtaining medical assistance under the French system. The booklet covers what you must pay for and how to reclaim any refundable charges, and is available through your doctor's surgery.

Chemist shops, *pharmacies*, are marked with a green cross, and can often deal with minor ailments and injuries, or give advice about where to go if additional help is needed.

What to do in an emergency

For emergency assistance dial 17 for Police, 18

for Fire Brigade, and, unless another number is given for Ambulance (usually on a notice to the right and about head height, above the telephone in public phone booths), dial 17 and ask the police for assistance. Most call-box telephones will have emergency and other information in English and other European languages.

In the case of an accident involving a third party, you should inform your insurer's French agent (address usually provided by the insurer, together with the International Vehicle Accident Report Form).

Messages about emergencies at home

Members of families touring abroad can be informed of serious illness in the family by courtesy of the BBC. In an emergency contact RAC Travel Information at Croydon, Tel: (01345) 333222, who will make arrangements for a message to be transmitted in the relevant country.

BBC World Service Broadcasts

The BBC World Service broadcasts in English 24 hours a day. World news is broadcast, on the hour, on the following frequencies (in kHz).

Northern France
0500-0730 hrs – 6195, 3955, 648
0730-1600 hrs – 12095, 9760, 648
1600-2230 hrs – 12095, 9410, 6195
Southern France
0500-0730 hrs – 9410, 6195, 3955
0730-1600 hrs – 15070, 12095, 9760
1600-2230 hrs – 12095, 9410, 6195

Telephoning the UK

Delete the first zero of the home number you are calling. Begin by dialling 19 44, then continue with the rest of the number (minus the first zero).

Most telephone booths use cards (*télécartes*) which can be bought at post offices or tobacconist shops. Post offices are open 0800-1900 Monday-Friday, and 0800-1200 on Saturday. Away from the larger towns they may close for about 1½ hours at lunchtime.

CONVERSION CHART

1 kilogram (1,000grams) = 2.2lbs
1 litre = 1¾ pints
4.5 litres = 1 gallon
1.6 kilometres = 1 mile
1.094 metres = 1 yard
1 hectare = 2½ acres (approx)
20°C = 68°F (°C x 1.8) + 32

WALKING IN BRITTANY

Walking is a popular sport in France and most of the footpath network, especially the well-used paths, is kept reasonably clear and way-marked.

Waymarking is by white/red horizontal stripes and a route number for Grandes Randonnées (GRs), long distance footpaths. Local routes are waymarked in yellow stripes, or other symbols. A waymark turned through right-angles means turn right (or left) at the next junction. If it has a line or cross drawn through it, it means 'do not go this way' (look for another waymark nearby indicating a turning).

Brittany has a number of GR long distance routes. The GR 34, which follows the coast along the Côtes d'Armor, from Mont St Michel to the Pointe du Raz, is the basis of a number of the coastal walks in this guide. There are also a number of inland GR circuits such as the Tour des Monts d'Arrée (GR 380), part of which is briefly used on Walk 22 (Ménez-Mikel). Other shorter local routes are circuits of towns and special features.

Using this guide

The walks in this guide are comparatively short and suitable for family groups and individuals of all ages. Most are conveniently close to popular holiday areas and start and finish at a car park, or near good roadside parking. Mention is made of nearby restaurants, or food shops where you can buy everything for a picnic.

Public toilets are few and far between in rural Brittany, but it is normally acceptable to use bar or café facilities, especially if you make a small purchase.

Almost all of the walks in this guide use clearly defined and well-used footpaths, but if in doubt, return to the last recognisable direction feature and start again.

Boots are not essential for these walks, but strong footwear should be worn. Not only will they be safer on stony paths, but more comfortable in the long run. Trainers with a thick patterned sole are ideal. Wear lightweight clothing, but make sure it protects against the sun. A light waterproof carried in a rucksack guards against unexpected showers. Also carry a small first aid kit which should contain an insect repellant. A water-based drink is another useful item to carry and prevents the danger of dehydration on a hot day.

Simple rules for walking in Brittany

1. Brittany has some of the fastest rising tides in the world. Do not be tempted to walk along the beach unless there is a safe way off.
2. Walk along the left-hand side of roads facing oncoming traffic.
3. Take your time. Hopefully the weather is warmer than you are normally used to, and in any case you could miss some interesting scene, or pretty view, by rushing.
4. Unless already open, shut all gates after going through them.
5. Respect growing crops, including hay grass, by keeping to the recognised route.
6. Protect wildlife, do not pick flowers or disturb nesting birds.
7. If it rains, be careful on muddy paths, especially when going downhill.
8. Do not try to make friends with farm dogs; their one purpose in life is to act as guardians!
9. Rabies is endemic in France and domestic animals are usually vaccinated. While the chances of contracting the disease are very slim, avoid contact with wild creatures while in the countryside.
10. Lock car doors and make sure that all windows are closed. Like in Britain, theft from unattended cars is a major problem in France.

HOTELS AND CAMPING

Hotels are classified by the French Government 'star' ratings, which range from the top of the range 'four-star L', through three lower grades to 'one star' category. Stars are awarded on the basis of the number of facilities in relation to the number of bedrooms, but do not necessarily indicate any recommendation of quality. In fact 'one or two-star' family-run hotels are frequently better places to stay than in the impersonable high-class establishments.

All hotels are obliged to show their room rates, which are per room and not for each person. Many smaller hotels include breakfast with the room rate. Menus, if the hotel has a restaurant, are also displayed, either beside the entrance, or next to the reception desk. Unless you have booked in advance, it is normal practice to examine the room before agreeing to take it.

Hotel bookings can be made through the local tourist office who will probably make a small charge.

The *Bienvenue à la Ferme* label, on the silhouette of a butterfly at the entrance to a farm, indicates that it offers rooms and board vetted and approved by the Gîtes de France organisation.

Not only will the accommodation and food be to a high standard, but the farm will also have recreational facilities and will be in an attractive setting. Children are always welcome and often encouraged to help with the animals.

Gîtes d'Hote (bed and breakfasts) are an inexpensive form of accommodation. Frequently in private houses, they are a pleasant way of getting to know the local people.

Many visitors prefer to self cater, and the range of rented accommodation is enormous, ranging from *châteaux*, to simple farmhouses or rural cottages, known as *gîtes*.

Camping can be through a pre-booked holiday organisation, or at one of the well-equipped sites throughout Brittany. As with hotels, a star rating indicates the number of facilities. Brittany has over 800 camp sites, ranging from 'four-star' top of the scale, which will have shops, swimming pools, tennis courts, marked pitches, laundry rooms and hot showers, to 'no-stars', which will only have very basic amenities.

Sources of useful information for booking holiday accommodation

Logis de France – book listing reasonably priced family-run hotels. Available from bookshops, or the French Government Tourist Office, 178 Piccadilly, London W1V 0AL.

Château Accueil – details of châteaux owners offering accommodation. Available from the French Government Tourist Office.

French Country Welcome – 14,000 B&B addresses. From Gîtes de France, 178 Piccadilly, London W1V 0AL.

Guide Michelin (Red Guide) – comprehensive information about towns and places to visit, as well as hotel and restaurant recommendations. Also lists garage telephone numbers. Available at most bookshops.

FURTHER USEFUL ADDRESSES

French Government Tourist Office
178 Piccadilly
London W1V 0AL   Tel: (0171) 491 7622

Brittany Chamber of Commerce
31 Seward St
London EC1V 3PA   Tel: (0171) 490 5579

Brittany Direct Holidays
– (inclusive holiday packages)
362 Sutton Common Road
Sutton
Surrey SM3 9PL   Tel: (0181) 641 6060

Matthews Holidays
– (travel inclusive mobile home holidays)
8 Bishopsmead Parade
East Horsley
Leatherhead
Surrey KT24 6RP   Tel: (01483) 284044

French Character Cottages
– (holiday cottages and villas)
8 Market Passage
Cambridge CB2 3AR   Tel: (01223) 35077

Bridgewater Travel
– (holiday villas, farmhouses and gîtes)
217 Monton Road
Monton
Manchester M30 9PN   Tel: (0161) 707 8547

France Accueil Hotels (UK) Ltd
– (hotel accommodation)
Westfield House
Bratton Road
Westbury
Wiltshire BA13 3EP   Tel: (01373) 824490

Gordon Holidays
– (rented accommodation)
118 Kidmore End Road
Emmer Green
Reading
Berks RG4 8SL   Tel: (01734) 472524

Fédération Français de la Randonnée Pédestre
64 Rue de Gergovie
75014 Paris   Tel: (010 33) 45 453102
(for information about the French GR network)

France Information Line
– Tel: (0891) 244123 (Calls cost 49p/minute peak rate; 39p/minute off peak). Free motorway maps, reference guide etc.

Logis de France
– (association of 340 family-run hotels)
Fédération Bretagne
4 Quai Thomas
35260 Cancale

LOCAL TOURIST OFFICES

Write to: 'Office de Tourisme' (followed by place name and address):

51 Avenue de la Plage, 29950 BENODET

BP 411, 29226 BREST Cedex

29226 CARANTEC

14 Avenue des Druids, 56340 CARNAC

6 Rue de l'Horloge, 22100 DINAN

BP 140, 35802 DINARD Cedex

Boulevard de la Mer, 22430 ERQUY

BP 14, 29170 FOUESNANT

La Grande Abbaye, 22240 FRÉHEL

22120 HILLION

22700 JUGON les LACS

BP 211, 22402 LAMBALLE Cedex

Les Quais, 22300 LANNION

BP 56, 56470 La TRINITÉ sur MER

Place des Otages, 29250 MORLAIX

BP 54, 22700 PERROS-GUIREC

BP 125, 22370 PLÉNEUF VAL ANDRÉ

22560 PLEUMEUR BODOU

BP 2, 22240 PLURIEN

BP 97, QUIBERON

Pont de Nemours, 35000 RENNES

BP 40, 29680 ROSCOFF

Place de Charles de Gaulle, 22380 St CAST Le GUIDO

Esplanade St Vincent, 35400 St MALO

22560 TREBEURDEN

BP 27 22730 TREGASTEL

22220 TRÉGUIER

1 Rue Theirs, 56000 VITRE

Other Tourist Office addresses

PAYS BIGOUDEN, BP 41, 29120 PONT L'ABBÉ

PAYS D'ACCUEIL DES ENCLOS ET MONTS D'ARRÉE, 12 Avenue Foch, 29402 LANDI-VISAU

PAYS DU HAUT LEON, Place de l'Evèché, 29250 ST POL DE LEON

RELAIS & CHÂTEAUX, Castel Clara, 56360 BELLE ÎLE EN MER

SEM PORT-RHU, Place de l'Enfer, 29100 DOUARNENEZ

GROUPEMENT TOURISTIQUE DES PAYS DE MORLAIX ET DES MONTS D'ARRÉE, BP6, 29201 MORLAIX Cedex

Walk 1
ROZ-SUR-COUESNON

5 km (3 miles)   Moderate

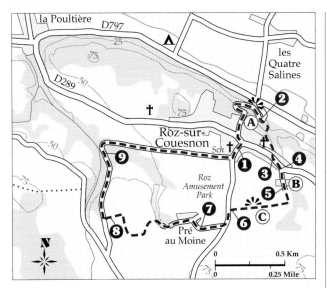

This is a walk around a sleepy village, perched high above rich farmland reclaimed from the sea, in the far north of Brittany. A view of St Michael's Mount comes early in the walk, followed by quaint by-ways and gently meandering tracks around nearby fields and woodland.

There are a couple of bar/restaurants offering simple, but good value fare; also a pâtisserie and a small grocery store.

How to get there: South of the D155/D797, St Malo to Pontorson coastal road, about 10 km (6 miles) from the latter.

Route description

❶ The walk starts by the side of the church, where there is usually ample parking space. Turn left and walk past the Bar Hamelin, then continue ahead at the road junction to follow the road signposted *Pays de Dol, Circuit Touristique*. Go downhill beyond the last houses.

❷ Where the road bends left at the bottom of a double hair-pin, and within sight of the main road, turn right on to a narrow woodland track. Follow this track uphill, then bear right on a footpath to climb past two small reservoirs. Beyond the upper reservoir a bet-ter path winds between a group of cottages.

❸ On reaching the road turn left at an ancient calvary cross and walk towards the village hall. (Modern building to the right and above the road).

❹ Turn right by the laundry well, along a farm lane, following the white waymark spots of the *Circuit Panoramique et Historique de Roz*. Continue past farm buildings.

❺ About 100 metres beyond the farm, the track approaches woodland. Turn right away from the trees, following white waymarks, along a narrow shaded path between fields. The path can be boggy where it is below field level, but drier ground can usually be found on the right of the path.

❻ Turn left at the road and almost immediately go to the right along a road signposted to *Pré au Moine*.

❼ Walk through the hamlet and go past the entrance to the Roz amusement park. Follow the track swinging right around the far edge of a small pine wood. Go down into a shallow valley and to the left of a small boating lake. Bear left away from the head of the lake to follow white waymarks uphill and along a tree-shaded path.

❽ Where the path joins a narrow road, turn right and walk downhill through woodland.

❾ Follow the road around a right-hand bend, then uphill with woodland on the right and small fields to the left, into the outskirts of Roz-sur-Couesnon. On reaching the village school, turn left along the street to reach the church.

Points of interest

Ⓐ Admire the view from the small public park on the right. Beyond is the wide sweep of St Michael's Bay, with the famous abbey standing on an almost perfect cone of rock projecting 78m (256ft) above the huge expanse of sands uncovered at low tide. Reputed to be the scene of a battle between St Michael and Satan, the abbey was founded in AD708 by Bishop Aubert of Avranches. The rocky mound and its church was once surrounded by an extensive forest, but changes in sea level inundated the forest and isolated the mount.

Ⓑ The water tank to the left of the track is a communal open-air laundry.

Ⓒ The view across the fields is of Roz-sur-Couesnon nestling around its venerable church.

Walk 2
POINTE DU GROUIN

5 km (3 miles)   Easy

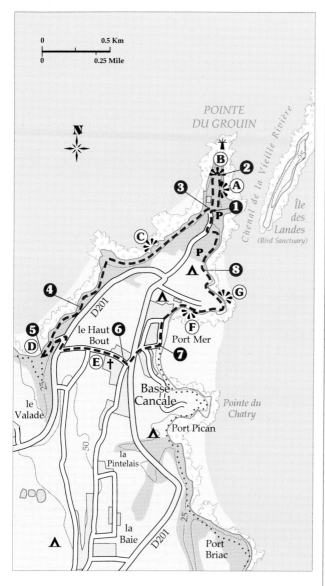

A stroll along high rocky clifftops covered in wild flowers. Offers views of off-shore islands and the ever-changing seascape of St Michael's Bay. A concrete gun emplacement, a grim relic of World War 2, is used as an information feature. Conveniently marking the half-way point, Port Mer, a pleasant seaside village, nestles beside a sheltered sandy bay. This makes an ideal stopping place, either for refreshment or to admire the view, or watch the skilful antics of sail board enthusiasts.

There is a restaurant near the lighthouse at the tip of the point and also crêperies, bars and cafés in Port Mer.

How to get there: North of Cancale by the D 201, or by the same road along the coast north-east from St Malo. Park at the road end near the point.

Route description

❶ From the car park, follow the gravel path past the front of the hotel and coastguard station to reach the narrow rocky Pointe du Grouin.

❷ Return to the hotel after visiting the point, then bear right to reach the path which follows the western edge of the peninsula.

❸ Continue to follow the clifftop path, winding around the tops of rocky gullies.

❹ Take heed of the short diversion and turn left to avoid stonework supporting an unstable section of the cliff. Follow the pavement for about 35m (38yds), then turn right to rejoin the undulating coastal path.

❺ Bear left above the beach, away from the shore to follow its access track climbing up to the road. Cross with care, diagonally right and then go left along a narrow lane across the peninsula.

❻ Left at the road junction and follow a side road down to the main road. Again cross with care, half left and then half right, to go down to the minor road opposite, signposted to *Plage de*

Port Mer. Walk down this to the sandy bay.

❼ Follow the sea front road until it makes a sharp left uphill. Turn right at the bend to follow a clifftop path below a group of houses (and waymarked by the white and red stripes of the GR 34 long distance trail).

❽ Bear right below the camp site and go down a short flight of steps, but ignore further steps to the right giving access to the beach, unless the tide is out. Continue to follow the cliff-edge path in and out of clumps of gorse bushes and blackthorns, all the way back to the car park.

Points of interest

Ⓐ Viewpoint. The concrete gun emplacement is a relic of Hitler's grandiose, but useless, "Atlantic Wall", futilely designed to deter Allied invasion. There is another emplacement still with its gun impotently covering the beach of Port Mer, which is unofficially, but aptly, used as a waste bin. The one near Pointe du Grouin now serves as an Interpretive Centre with details of the many sea birds living or breeding on and around the nearby cliffs. The narrow Île des Landes, opposite and across the dangerous currents of the aptly named Chenal de la Vieille Rivière (the channel of the old river), is protected as a bird reserve. Attractive wild flowers, including several unusual varieties, grow in the salt-laden air.

Ⓑ Viewpoint. Pointe du Grouin, jutting far out into Mont St Michel Bay, makes a perfect vantage point. The mount and its abbey are to the south-east, standing in miles of golden sands at low tide. To the left of the mount is the uninhabited rock of Rocher de Tombelaine. Together with Mont St Michel and Mont Dol on the mainland to your right, these are the remains of ancient volcanic stumps. Breton legend links them with a battle between the devil and Saint Michael. Legends occur linking St Michael with rocky places all over Europe (viz: St Michael's Mount in Cornwall), and it is possible that these sites were used by the followers of a pagan religion who were converted to Christianity.

Slightly closer to hand, and on the limits of sand uncovered at low tide, row upon row of *buchots*, palings stuck into the sand, are used for growing shellfish. Harvesting, for one can hardly call it fishing, is done from tractors and amphibious vehicles at low tide.

The stately progress of ferries and local fishing boats busily winding in and out of the islets and sea-washed rocks of *la Manche* (English Channel) offer a constant diversion.

Ⓒ Viewpoint. The surrounding rocks of the coast are mostly granite, the underlying strata of Brittany. When worn, granite forms a pale gold sand, giving the sea its gentle turquoise effect on a sunny day.

Jet black cormorants, under-sea fishing birds, can often be seen on nearby rocks, standing motionless with outstretched wings, drying their feathers after a spell under water.

Ⓓ Being the half-way point of the walk, the sheltered bay makes an ideal stopping place, either for a bathe or maybe a picnic.

Ⓔ Stop a moment to admire the tiny wayside chapel of Notre Dame de Haute Bout. Wayside shrines and fishermen's chapels such as this one are an attractive feature of the Brittany coast.

Ⓕ Viewpoint. Port Mer's sheltered bay offers safe anchorage for both pleasure craft and fishing boats. Its safe beach is popular with windsurfers or the handful of holidaymakers who have discovered its almost hidden charms. To the south is Pointe de la Chaîne, reached by a clifftop footpath once used by coastguards and revenue men in the days when smuggling was a more innocent occupation. It was from secluded bays such as Port Mer that *"brandy for the parson, baccy for the clerk"* set sail under cover of darkness for England's shores.

The fishing port of Cancale is out of sight to the south of Pointe de la Chaîne. Its seafront restaurants offer a mouthwatering variety of seafood dishes and other traditional Breton fare.

Ⓖ Viewpoint. Branches of pine trees frame an attractive view of the Île des Landes and, at the turn of tide, swiftly flowing currents through the Chenal de la Vieille Rivière, between the narrow island and the Pointe du Grouin.

Walk 3
CAP FRÉHEL

8 km (5 miles)   Moderate

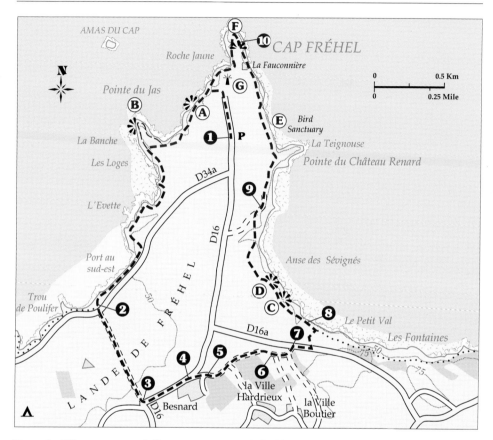

Dramatic clifftop scenery and distant seascapes are linked by gentle moors and wind-sculpted wood-land on this walk at the tip of a long peninsula that was once the home of a giant. Sea birds float easily on updraughts in the rocky gullies, or nest on narrow ledges on the precipitous crags.

Cap Fréhel, being the high point of the walk, is deliberately left to the end. The cape is considered to be one of Brittany's most picturesque headlands, and certainly makes a stupendous viewpoint. Red, black and grey cliffs of the cape fall vertically for over 70m (230ft) into the ever-surging waves. Cap Fréhel has always been a danger to shipping and its lighthouse is both a constant warning and a navigational aid.

There is a small restaurant, *La Fauconnière*, near the lighthouse and an old farmhouse hotel, the *Relais de Fréhel*, about half way round the walk.

How to get there: About 21 km (13 miles) north-east of Erquy by way of the D786 (St Malo road) to Plurien and the D34/D34a coast road, or the D16 from St Aide, again on the D786. There is a large car park at the road end adjacent to the lighthouse.

Route description

❶ Leave the car park and walk towards the lighthouse and turn left to follow the rocky clifftop path for about 2.5 km (1½ miles).

❷ Where the cliff path joins the main road cross with care, and turn left to follow an unsurfaced track across the open moor. Head towards a group of houses on the skyline.

❸ Bear left at the staggered crossroads and walk along the surfaced road for about 350m (217yds), past several large houses as far as a road fork by a signpost to *Relais de Fréhel*.

❹ Fork right to walk down the lane, past the entrance to the Relais (a recommended lunch stop), then ahead at a signpost indicating 'no through road' (*voie sans issue*).

❺ Ignoring further turnings to the right or left, follow the grassy track, slightly uphill between sheltered fields and rough woodland. Where the track turns right into a field, continue forwards on what soon becomes a grassy footpath.

❻ Over the top of a low rise, the path widens into a track again. Keep to the left at two track junctions within 120m (131yds) of each other, then walk down to the road and turn right.

❼ About 150m (164yds) along the road, look for a faint path on the left and follow it, winding between gorse bushes for a short distance until it descends the open moor to reach a wider path along the coast. Turn left here.

❽ Continue to follow the cliff edge, climbing where necessary to cross a dry gully, and follow occasional white/red waymarks.

❾ Bear right on reaching a wider track, following it until the white/red waymarks leave it in favour of a further stretch of coastal path.

❿ On reaching the point at Cap Fréhel, pause to admire the view before turning left to follow a wide path up to, and beyond, the lighthouse, then bear left to reach the car park.

Points of interest

Ⓐ Viewpoint for the dramatic sea cliffs of the Pointe du Jas where sea birds nest on what seem impossibly narrow ledges and gracefully swoop down towards the sea in search of food. The intervening moorland is interspersed with pockets of wild flowers, some of them quite rare, and with sheltered hollows where small birds like finches and buntings nest in spring.

Ⓑ Viewpoint. Divert to the right past WW2 fortifications and on to the Pointe du Jas. The view is to the west across the Baie de St Brieuc towards the sandy shores of the Côte de Goelo coast and the magical Île de Bréhat.

Ⓒ Viewpoint. The view to the right, beyond the rocks of Les Fontaines, is of a dramatic rocky headland topped by Fort Lalatte. A fairy-tale castle of towers and massive pink stone encircling walls, it was begun in the thirteenth century, but improved in Napoleonic times by the military architect Sébastien Vaubin, who was responsible for the design of the old citadel town of St Malo. Entered by a double drawbridge over natural clefts in the rock, the castle is open to the public. A little to the right of the fort, and visible on a clear day from this viewpoint, is Gargantua's Finger, an impressive menhir supposedly left by a mythical giant. He is supposed to be buried on Cap Fréhel with his head near Fort Lalatte and his feet at St Suliac 25 km (15½ miles) away!

Menhirs are standing stones, the word means 'long stone' in Breton. There are literally thousands of similar ancient relics dotted about Brittany; menhirs, dolmens (massive blocks supported by smaller standing stones), stone circles, aligned rows and tumuli mounds. Their purpose is lost in the mists of time, but all are surrounded by a mystical aura. Many stand within the confines of Christian churches, leading to the suggestion that they may have had a pagan use. Several of these ancient features are visited on other walks in this guide.

Ⓓ The view ahead is of the Pointe du Château Renard (the fox's den), red cliffs flecked with black and grey, giving shelter to a tiny unnamed harbour at its foot.

Ⓔ The cliffs between Pointe du Château Renard and the *La Fauconnière* Restaurant have been designated as a bird sanctuary, a popular nesting place for migratory and local birds every spring.

Ⓕ Cap Fréhel. Follow the path around the cliff edge, but not too close! This is one of the most spectacular viewpoints on the Brittany coast. From it can be seen most of the Emerald Coast, from Bréhat island to Pointe du Grouin near Cancale, and on a clear day, the Channel Islands.

Ⓖ There have been three lighthouses on Cap Fréhel. Climb the 145 steps of the modern lighthouse in order to enjoy an even better view.

St Malo sailors had a special affinity with Cap Fréhel: their wedding vows were automatically suspended as they passed the point on outward voyages, but woe betide any who thought this applied when homeward bound!

Walk 4
PLAGE DE LA VILLE BERNEUF   7 km (4 miles)   Easy

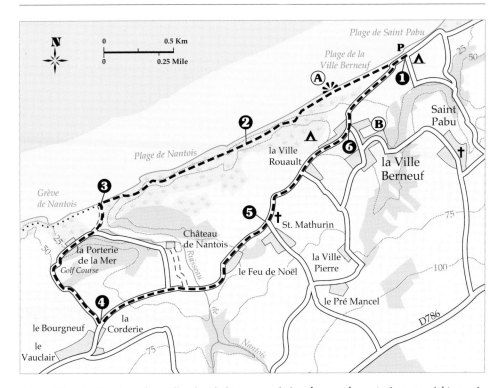

Tranquil farmland, untamed woodland and glorious sandy beaches are the main features of this gentle stroll. The walk can be combined with a visit to the nearby Château Bien Assis.

The only place of refreshment is the small crêperie near the camp site of St Pabu, but there are many restaurants in nearby Erquy or Pléneuf-Val-André.

How to get there: Side roads off the D34 or D786, about half way between Erquy and Pléneuf-Val-André. Park next to the beach in front of the St Pabu camp site.

Route description
N.B. Do not attempt to vary the walk by using the beach between Points ❶-❸ when the tide is coming in as there are no safe ways off the beach.
❶ Follow the coastal path to the left, at first beside a row of tall cedar trees along the springy turf of a grassy path.
❷ The path continues across a steep, scrub-covered hillside, sometimes close to the beach, and at other points climbing high to avoid small promontories.

❸ Above the shore and in close proximity to a ruined house, turn left and climb the access track, beside the golf course on the right. Where the track joins a surfaced lane, follow it with fairways of the golf course on either side.
❹ Turn left at the junction with a minor road. Follow it through undulating farmland and small stretches of woodland; past the entrance to the Château de Nantois (private). Continue along the road through a sleepy hamlet with the attractive name of le Feu de Noël.

❺ Left by the chapel of St Mathurin to follow the road signposted to the *Plage de la Ville Berneuf*.
❻ Keep to the left through the village, downhill past the entrance to a camp site to reach the beach.

Points of interest
Ⓐ Viewpoint. Across the bay is the fishing port of Erquy. To your left is the headland sheltering the resort of Val-André and the bird sanctuary rock of le Verdelet.
Ⓑ The village of la Ville Berneuf has several interesting stone-built farmhouses and cottages.

Walk 5
POINTE DES GUETTES

8 KM (5 miles)   Easy

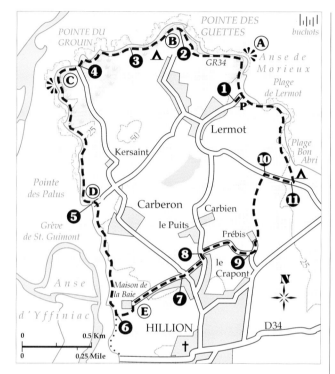

⑥ At a footpath sign, turn left to climb a short flight of steps to reach a field path. Go to the right of the Maison de la Baie, and follow its access drive, then go uphill past a line of houses.

⑦ At the road junction cross over to follow a track waymarked with yellow arrows on a red square. At the next road turn left for about 60m (65yds).

⑧ Turn right along a farm lane, signposted to *la Pierre Blanche*.

⑨ Turn left and follow an access drive as far as the house. Do not enter its yard, but bear right as indicated by a footpath sign leading to the beach.

⑩ At the road turn right, downhill for 200m (219yds) towards the coast.

⑪ Turn left above the camp site and follow the path around a small headland back to the car park.

Points of interest

Ⓐ Viewpoint across the mouth of Gouessant river where row upon row of *buchots* grow shellfish. To the north-east are the sands of Val-André, considered to be the finest beach in Brittany.

Ⓑ The ruined look-out post is a relic of the WW2 'Atlantic Wall.'

Ⓒ Viewpoint. St Brieuc, to the left across the sands of the Yffiniac estuary, stands on a plateau between the rives Gouët and Gouedic, each being crossed by high viaducts. Markets have been held in Place du Matry, next to the cathedral, since medieval times, and there is also a fair in September.

Ⓓ A well at the road end once supplied visiting sailing ships with fresh water.

Ⓔ Maison de la Baie Field Study Centre deals with subjects related to the river estuary. There is a small exhibition which is usually open to the public, and a small restaurant.

Here is a gentle stroll around a sheltered headland. An excellent vantage point for views along the coast; St Brieuc can be seen to the south-west, and in the opposite direction is the Gouessant estuary. The coast stretches to the north-east, where Pointe de Pléneuf shelters the glorious sands of Val-André.

Refreshments can be found at Hillion, a little to the south of the walk, where there are one or two small bar/restaurants, and also drinks and snacks at the Maison de la Baie Field Study Centre.

How to get there: North of Yffiniac on the D80 to Hillion, then by a minor road north to Lermot; park at Plage de Lermot. Access from the N12 St Brieuc/Rennes road is via the D81 St René interchange, then D712 in the direction of Yffiniac to join the D80 at le Dernier Sou.

Route description

① From the Plage de Lermot car park walk towards the beach and turn left to follow the cliff path waymarked with the white/red stripes of the GR 34.

② Keeping to the path, follow the coast leftwards around the Pointe des Guettes.

③ Cross a flight of steps leading to the beach and continue ahead along the cliff-top path.

④ Where the path crosses the end of an access lane walk on, still following the white/red stripes.

⑤ Cross the beach access track, to continue along the cliff path.

19

Walk 6
CHAOS DU GOUËT

8 km (5 miles)   Moderate

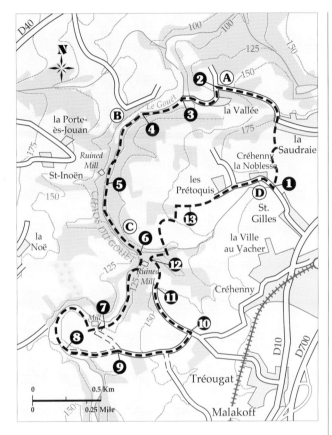

The word 'Chaos' in the title simply means boulder-filled gorge. The walk is mostly along well-defined paths beside a tree-shaded river and passes the ruins of three long-abandoned mills.

As the nearest source of refreshment is at St Julien, about 2 km (1¼ miles) north of the walk, a drink and a light snack should be carried.

How to get there: South-east from St Brieuc by the D700 to the Malakoff Interchange; north on the D790, St Julien road, for about 1.5 km (1 mile), then turn left on a minor road into St Gilles. Park on the grass verge, about 150m (164yds) beyond the village, before the road turns left beyond a restored farmhouse.

Route description

❶ Facing away from St Gilles, turn right and away from the road. Follow a grassy track until it meets a surfaced road. Turn left and walk downhill on the road.

❷ Turn left at the road junction, down into a wooded valley, and bear left within sight of the river.

❸ Follow a riverside path upstream.

❹ Ignore a path going right to cross a stone clapper bridge. Continue beside the river and walk beneath the shade of tall trees.

❺ Again ignore a second bridge and path to your right, and walk forwards into the narrowing gorge.

❻ Bear right to cross a side stream and follow occasional waymarks, still upstream.

❼ Cross an access drive and follow the path to the left of a restored mill.

❽ Turn left and uphill on joining a farm track.

❾ Ignoring side tracks, follow the lane ahead and steadily uphill between fields.

❿ Turn left at the junction and walk down the road.

⓫ At the road end, turn half right and go down the sunken tree-shaded path.

⓬ Turn sharp right at the woodland path junction. Bear left to cross a little stream and climb the steep opposite side of the wooded valley.

⓭ Above the forest, the path improves and eventually becomes a surfaced lane which leads past houses to the car.

Points of interest

Ⓐ A solitary menhir stands amongst newly-planted trees on the right of the road junction.

Ⓑ The ancient stone clapper bridge on the right leads to the ruins of a mill.

Ⓒ The Chaos du Gouët. Massive glacier-borne rocks fill the gorge, making the river froth and boil in its passage beneath and around them.

Ⓓ The restored farmhouse of Créhenny la Noblesse, on the left, is an interesting example of a Breton 'longhouse'.

Walk 7
LE PALUS & POINTE DE PLOUHA
6 km (3.5 miles)   Easy

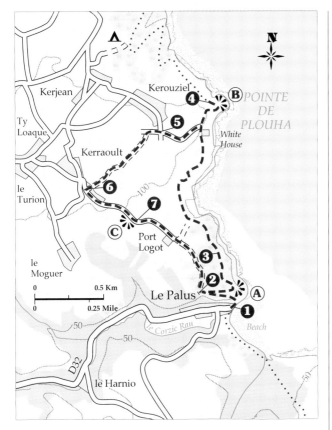

Route description

❶ Climb the 42 steps on the seaward side of the *Homardine Restaurant*, then follow the steep path up on to the gorse and broom-covered cliffs.

❷ Following white/red way-marks, bear right at the footpath junction, then along the well-maintained clifftop path.

❸ Ignoring any side turns, follow the cliff for about 1.5 km (1 mile) until a large white, clifftop house comes into view, a little to your right. Bear left, then right, along its boundary fence, then walk on towards the viewpoint on Pointe de Plouha.

❹ Retrace your steps as far as the white house and follow its access drive to the right.

❺ Go forwards at the crossroads to bear left after 80m (87yds), and then walk along a gravel-surfaced farm lane.

❻ Go through the farmyard and onwards as far as a road to make a left turn.

❼ Follow the road to its end, then ahead by the track which starts beyond the last houses. Walk through sheltering woodland to join the outward path. Turn right at the path junction and walk downhill into Le Palus.

N.B. Take care going down the steep path which is made slippery by loose stones.

Points of interest

Ⓐ Viewpoint along the coast towards Pointe du Bec de Vir and the bay of St Brieuc.

Ⓑ Viewpoint looking east towards the Cherbourg peninsula, where, on a clear day, you can see the Channel Islands. Escaping Allied airmen shot down over France were ferried out from a beach near this point.

Ⓒ Viewpoint westwards across the lush farmlands of the Côtes d'Armour département of Brittany.

On this walk gorse and bracken-covered clifftops, rocky headlands and gentle seascapes contrast with lush farmland and sunny villages inland in an ever-changing panorama of tranquility. The walk is from Le Palus, a pleasant little family resort beside a sheltered beach at the mouth of a woodland valley. With one steep climb from the beach, the walk then follows the coast to a high rocky promontory before meandering inland and back to Le Palus.

Anyone with energy to spare could extend the walk from either Pointe de Plouha or Le Palus, by using the network of tracks in the area.

Le Palus has a couple of restaurants and a crêperie; the fish dishes at the *Homardine* are especially recommended.

How to get there: D786 to Plouha, then the D32 valley road east to Le Palus. Park at the road end beside the beach.

Walk 8
ÎLE DE BRÉHAT

13 km (8 miles)   – maximum –   Easy

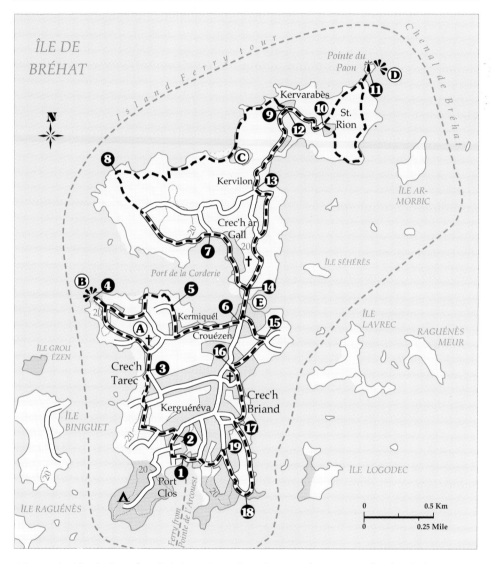

A low rocky island of weathered pink granite and sandstone with an average height a little over 15m (49ft) above sea level, the Île de Bréhat has the added attraction of being virtually traffic free.

Reached by a 15-minute ferry ride from the Pointe de l'Arcouest, the island is a stroller's paradise. The walk described here is a rough figure-of-eight which can easily be split into two shorter walks.

Île de Bréhat is actually two islands. Linked by a bridge, the Pont ar Prad, the northern island is the least inhabited and probably offers the greatest scope for 'away from it all' wandering.

Île de Bréhat was once an advanced fortress in the defence of France and was attacked several times during Napoleonic wars by English warships. A small citadel set amongst pinewoods in the south of the main island, le Goaréva, still guards Port Clos, the remaining link with a time when English visitors were less welcome than now!

The island has a number of small cafés and family-run restaurants, mostly in the main town of Île de Bréhat, or near the landing stage at Port Clos.

How to get there: D789 from Paimpol to the embarkation point at Pointe de l'Arcouest. Parking is usually plentiful on either side of the road end.

Ferries: All year round from Pointe de l'Arcouest to Port Clos. Departure is half past each hour and returns on the hour. Crossing time 15 minutes.

Summer only from: la Roche Jagu (1hr 15min). St Quay-Portrieux (1hr 30min). Binic (1hr 50min). Erquy (2hr). Jersey (3hr). Guernsey (3hr 30min).

N.B. All sailings are subject to weather conditions.

There is a camp site near the ancient citadel on the tree-covered point at le Goaréva on the western arm of Port Clos Bay.

Route description

❶ From the ferry landing at Port Clos, walk up to the road and turn left past white-walled cottages and tropical gardened villas. Take the right turn at the T-junction, then over the cross-roads and follow the narrow road bearing right.

❷ Turn left, and left again after 50m (55yds), towards the coast, then fork right at the next junction. Walk towards a line of trees and turn right. Follow the road, past scattered houses to a fork. Turn left and almost immediately right, along a narrow track past a T-junction and towards the sandy bay of Crec'h Tarec.

❸ Join a slightly wider lane and follow it around the bay towards the chapel on a slight rise ahead. Bear left at the junction below the chapel, then right at the next fork. Walk on, ignoring side turnings towards the narrow, scrub-covered point jutting into the open channel.

❹ Walk back from the point and bear left on to a lane passing a group of cottages. Carry on to the next junction and turn left again, towards the bay. Go forwards, past the house at the lane end and walk out on to the foreshore. Turn right and follow a footpath along the shoreline.

❺ Where the path meets a narrow road, turn left along it, past cottages and an old farmhouse.

❻ Turn left at the road junction and walk on to cross the bridge over the narrow channel dividing the island in two. Take the next fork left and follow the road around the bay.

❼ Left at the fork, on to an unsurfaced lane which gradually turns inland, winding between low hummocks to reach the northern shoreline.

❽ Turn right at the point and follow a grassy path above the shoreline for about 2 km (1¼ miles), past a small pond until the path joins a narrow road at the hamlet of Kervarabès.

❾ Follow the road left to its end by a cluster of houses at St Rion.

❿ Go forwards to follow a footpath across open scrub as far as the lighthouse on the rocky outcrop of Pointe du Paon.

⓫ Walk back about 200m (219yds) from the lighthouse and turn left at the path junction to follow the coast for 500m (310yds), then begin to bear right to reach the road and houses at pointer ❿. At the houses turn left, following the road around a sharp right-left bend towards the group of cottages at pointer ❾.

⓬ Still following the road, go past the tree-sheltered houses on the left and follow the road to a staggered crossroads.

⓭ Bear left, then right, along a farm lane until it meets the road again. Go forwards on this to the island bridge.

⓮ Cross the bridge, walk forwards to the next road junction and turn left.

⓯ Go left, then right, over the staggered cross roads, towards the sea and turn right to follow a track into the island's main village. Walk up to the square.

⓰ Turn left at the square, go past the church and down to the coast, then bear right inland again.

⓱ Left at the crossroads following the narrow road towards the tree-covered headland.

⓲ Go to the right with the road and walk inland between tiny fields and past a number of attractive villas.

⓳ Turn left down the narrow lane which winds its way back to the ferry landing stage.

Points of interest

Ⓐ The Chapelle St Michel sits on top of a high mound giving the finest view of the island.

Ⓑ Viewpoint. At low tide the tiny Île Modez is linked to the mainland by a huge expanse of rocky foreshore.

Ⓒ The brackish lake on the right attracts migrating waders and other seabirds.

Ⓓ Viewpoint. The lighthouse on Pointe du Paon looks out on to the open waters of la Manche.

Ⓔ At high (spring) tides, the sea fills the channel beneath the bridge cutting the island in two.

Walk 9
KERBORS

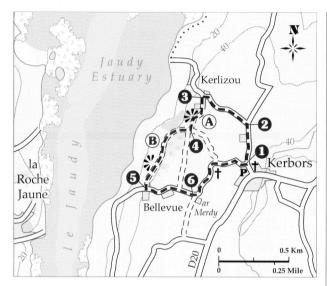

Anyone with a taste for the unusual should visit the Centre d'Étude et de Valorisation des Algues (CEVA), near Pleubian; a title for the study of industrial and culinary uses of seaweed!

The town of Tréguier sits on a high plateau above the confluence of the tiny Guindy river and the Jaudy, almost at the limit of navigable water. Its sheltered position makes Tréguier a perfect anchorage for pleasure craft of all sizes, and in summer the narrow estuary is full of a colourful array of sailing and powered boats. The pink granite spire of St Tudwal's cathedral soars high above the terraced streets of the ancient town. Its open lattice-worked structure, a common feature through Brittany, is designed to offer the minimum resistance to winter gales. The cathedral's sixty-eight windows were once filled with medieval stained glass, but they were lost through zealous vandalism during the Revolution. However, the modern replacement gives a beautifully warm glow and a worthwhile alternative. The gracefully columned Porte St-Jean on the north side of the cathedral leads to the tranquil peace of fifteenth-century cloisters. St Yves, a man of great legal wisdom and the patron saint of Brittany lawyers, is buried in Tréguier cathedral. Members of the legal profession march in stately procession every year on 19 May, the anniversary of his death. There is also a Pardon in

Motoring, even around somewhere as attractive as the Côtes de Granit Rose, the 'Pink Granite Coast' of the Côtes d'Armour, can become tedious, and a short walk is often a welcome break. This walk, which is from the tiny village of Kerbors, needs only an hour or so to complete, and is therefore an ideal way of filling the gap in a planned itinerary.

The walk starts in the centre of the sleepy village of Kerbors, beside its venerable church. A gentle stroll along farm lanes will take you out to views over the narrow Jaudy estuary, where luxury yachts and inshore fishing boats find safe anchorage. Commercially tended oyster beds, an important part of Brittany's marine economy, are sited amongst sheltered rocks or quiet bays. Part of a secluded corner of Brittany, away from the effects of Atlantic gales, the surrounding fields grow high-value crops such as early vegetables, soft fruit, artichokes and asparagus.

Inquisitive but friendly villagers in and around Kerbors will be interested in the rare visit of English-speaking visitors. There is a small bar-cum-village shop which acts as the focal point for everyday activities in Kerbors, and also a small crêperie. A visit to either, especially the shop, will inevitably lead to friendly banter with the locals.

Kerbors is about half way between Tréguier and Pleubian, amidst green fields high above the eastern bank of the Jaudy estuary. The fjord-like river, with the River Trieux to the east, has formed a long sandy spit, the Sillon de Talbert, at the tip of the Presqu'île Sauvage, the 'wild almost island', on a particulary dramatic stretch of the Côte de Granite Rose.

his honour, the Pardon des Pauvres, which is held on the third Sunday in May.

Ancient half-timbered houses surround the Place du Martray, and line the steep streets. Rue Renan leads down to the old town gates. The street is named after a Tréguier-born nineteenth-century philosopher who crossed swords with the Catholic church by declaring that Christ was simply a man of extraordinary abilities, rather than the son of God. There is a statue of Renan in the Place du Martray, and a museum devoted to his life close by.

How to get there: Leave the D786 Paimpol road, about half a kilometre (third of a mile) east of Tréguier. Drive north along the D20 (Pleubian road), through Trédarzec for five kilometres (three miles). Park either beside the church, or in the Place de la Mairie.

Route description

1 Take a little time exploring this sleepy little village before following the country road which winds between the church and the *Mairie* (town mayor's office). Walk on for about 320m (350yds), past occasional houses and an old farmhouse.

2 Turn left at a road junction and go down a farm lane set between high embankments covered with a profusion of wild flowers throughout the summer months.

3 At a T-junction, turn left opposite a farmhouse and walk down the narrow access lane. Beyond a modern house at the limit of the surfaced way, continue ahead along a rough cart track.

4 Go to the right at the staggered crosstracks. Walk on between open fields on the right and scrub bushland to your left.

5 Ignore the white/red waymarking indicating a right turn on entering the little hamlet of Bellevue and turn left to follow its access road uphill, past groups of stone cottages and more modern houses.

6 Follow the road turning left at a T-junction beside the farm of ar Merdy, then walk on beside flowery embankments and below open fields. Bear right as the road turns next to an old chapel and head for the spire of Kerbor's church directly ahead.

Points of interest

A Viewpoint. Across the vegetable garden of the attractive modern house with its modern collection of megalithic alignments. The view is of the scattered offshore rocks and islets guarding the mouth of the River Jaudy. Miles of golden sands offer enchantment to holidaymakers, and the wooden palings of man-made oyster beds will interest gourmets.

B Viewpoint. Looking across the fjord-like waters of the Jaudy to the safe anchorage and holiday villas below the village of la Roche Jaune. Around the village are tiny fields of rich soil, sheltered from the harsh Atlantic winter gales by stone boundary walls and high earth embankments. The walls provide an ideal environment for a multitude of wild flowers, birds and small mammals.

Walk 10
POINTE DU CHÂTEAU & CASTEL MEUR 8 km (5 miles) Easy

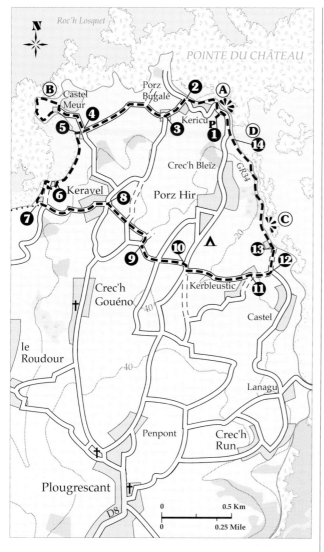

In summer it is hard to imagine the differences brought by weather patterns of the changing seasons. The low-lying coast of the Pointe du Château juts far out into a haphazard jumble of rocky tors and tiny green islands, where golden sands and a turquoise sea look so inviting and innocent.

The walk starts by a sheltered beach, follows the coast for a little way before moving inland through green fields contrasting the browns, greys, pink and bright reds of the outer rocks. A tiny island with one of the most scenically positioned houses in Brittany is connected to the mainland by a narrow causeway. This is the focal point of the walk. The way back is through lush fields and past farm settlements linking both coasts of the narrow headland.

On the way to Pointe du Château, the peninsula road goes through Plougrescant. Passing visitors cannot help but notice the curiously twisted steeple and sloping walls of its church. Dating from the tenth century, it is believed that the first church on this site was built by St Gonéry. He was a Celtic monk who brought Christianity to what was then a heathen land. Inside the church a stone trough, reputed to be the saint's coffin, is more likely to be the fireplace of the ship which brought him over to Brittany from Ireland. St Gonéry's skull is kept in a glass case in the chapel. It is carried in procession in a sedan chair-like vehicle each springtime, then by boat to the nearby Île Loaven where the saint's mother,

Jagged sea-washed granite outcrops lie in wait for unwary shipping entering the narrow anchorage of the Jaudy estuary. On a bland windless summer day, with the sun shining from an azure sky, they make an attractive division between the land and sea. But on a day with a wild south-westerly gale screaming off the Atlantic, the scene can conjure feelings akin to abject terror.

Eliboubane, is said to be buried. Vibrantly-coloured frescoes in the chapel depict Old Testament scenes. The paintings of Adam and Eve are particularly interesting. Originally painted nude, the figures were later 'clothed' as the originals were considered too daring for the innocent minds of the local peasantry! Some of the woodwork around the nave is carved in the wild scroll-work associated with the Celtic school of influence.

Refreshments can be found at the hotel/restaurant in Porz Hir or at several establishments in Plougrescant.

How to get there: D786 to Tréguier, then north on D8 through Plougiel to Plougrescant. Onwards by an unclassified road via Porz Hir to the small harbour east of Porz Bugalé. Parking space is available to the left of the road alongside the harbour.

Route description

❶ Facing the harbour, leave the car park and turn left along the road. Walk past a massive group of outcropping rocks, then go to the right towards the beach as indicated by an enamel footpath sign. Follow the coastal path through sedge-protected dunes on the tidal limit of the sandy bay.

❷ Leave the coast to join the narrow road which heads towards a farmhouse dominated by huge ivy-covered granite tors.

❸ Bear right at the farm to follow a side lane signposted to le Gouffre (the cave), and go between two almost identical rocky outcrops. Bear left at an indicator map of the area and skirt a line of tall pine trees.

❹ Go through the bus park and bear right, then go through a barrier to follow the traffic-free road

on to the tiny island of Castel Meur. There is no recognised footpath around the island. Simply wander at will, enjoying its charms and hidden rocky chasms before returning to the bus park.

❺ From the bus and car park, follow the road to the right for a short distance around the sandy bay, as far as the cottage on the right of the road. Go to the right around the side of the cottage and follow a narrow grassy path to the left of the beach and above the high water mark.

❻ Scramble through a jumble of rocks leading to a cottage nestling in the shelter of a huge rock which is on its seaward side. Go to the left of the cottage, along its access drive, then bear right on reaching a track junction. Head towards a house with three windows in the wall facing the track.

❼ Turn left at the house, uphill along the by-road and between fields leading to the scattered hamlet of Keravel.

❽ Go over a crossroads and follow the minor road opposite downhill for about 200m (219yds). Ignore any side tracks leading to fields or roadside cottages.

❾ Take the left fork at the junction and follow a narrow road winding uphill between meadows and small sheltered fields. Take the road opposite at the crossroads, go over the brow of the hill and begin to go steadily downhill.

❿ Turn right at the T-junction, then immediately left down a side road signposted, amongst other features, to the Plage de Varlen.

⓫ Go to the left at the lane junction, downhill towards the coast.

⓬ Follow a footpath sign left, along a side track heading downhill towards the beach.

⓭ At the lane end bear left around the front of a white-

painted stone cottage to follow a field path waymarked with the white/red stripes of the GR 34, above the high water mark.

⓮ Climb up to the road, turn right and follow it past the little harbour and back to the car park.

Points of interest

Ⓐ Viewpoint. Across the Jaudy estuary with its myriads of granite rocks and tiny islands surrounded by golden sands washed by a turquoise sea.

Ⓑ Castel Meur; the word 'castel' is the same as the Welsh for 'castle', proof of the linguistic links between these two Celtic nations. Castel is therefore an apt description for the massive jumble of rocks when viewed from this point. The cottage across the brackish lagoon has rightly been the subject of countless photographs and paintings. No matter how many times anyone might have seen its portrait, the first glimpse is one of absolute delight. Set between two massive granite outcrops, the setting can only be described as idyllic. Sheltered corners of the island are ideal for sunbathing or picnicking. For the more energetically inclined, the rocks are made for exploring and the little inlets for beachcombing. The gouffre (cave) is a narrow sea-filled defile on the far side of the rocky summit of the island. **Do not try to climb into it, because the rocks are slippery and the sea can surge through the narrow cleft without warning.**

Ⓒ Viewpoint. Looking out over the rocks and sand spits guarding the mouth of the Jaudy estuary. The largest island, Île d'Er ou Énez Terc'h, is only inhabited during the summer.

Ⓓ Kericu's attractive outcrop-sheltered harbour is worth exploring and can offer any number of subjects for amateur photographers.

Walk 11
ROCHES DE PLOUMANAC'H

3 km (2 miles)   Easy

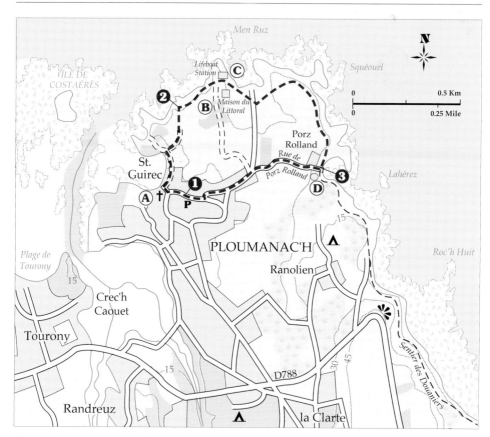

Strangely contorted and weather-worn rocks line the shores and coastal waters of the *Côtes de Granit Rose*, the 'Pink Granite Coast', but it is the rocks of Ploumanac'h which probably excite the greatest attention.

Although granite is an exceptionally hard rock which erodes slowly, it does have intrusions of quartz which weather more easily, leaving the characteristic tors and outcrops of this unique coast. The strange, weirdly-formed rocks stand above the shoreline, behind this one-time fishing village. Worn by the combined action of the waves, frost, wind and rain over countless millenia, each of the massive rocks has taken on an individual and original character. Many have been given names, like Napoleon's Hat, the Corkscrew, Death's Head, the Tortoises and the Witch, but it needs no stretch of the imagination, and can pass an amusing hour or so, wandering around the groups of rocks, deciding what each one looks like.

Set in a municipal park at the tip of the Trégastel peninsula, the rock-filled area of land is open for anyone to wander through, to picnic, or simply to admire 'Nature's Sculpture Gallery'.

Ploumanac'h began its life as a fishing port, but, being surrounded by sheltered beaches, it has grown into a pleasant holiday resort. The village is on the eastern side of an indented sandy bay opposite Trégastel Plage where the Grève Blanche, the white beach, is considered the best one in this district.

There is a sea-water aquarium in a series of caves to the north of the resort and near it is the statue of *Père Éternel* (Eternal Father), which looks out over a fine viewpoint.

The largest resort on the Trégastel peninsula is Perros-Guirec, to the south-east of Ploumanc'h, and it can be reached by extending this walk from Porz Rolland at the eastern end of the Municipal Park. A footpath, the *Sentier des Douaniers*, the old customs path, follows the coast to the Plage de Trestraou. In summer, boats sail from this crescent-shaped bathing beach to the bird sanctuary of les Sept Îles. Even though Perros-Guirec is a modern resort, it is built around a medieval church. Made from pink granite, the Romanesque structure is considered to be one of the most beautiful in Brittany. The town is also a centre for thalassotherapy, the sea-water treatment of medical problems. The use of sea water and seaweed is not new to Brittany, but thalassotherapy centres are a fairly new innovation.

Ploumanac'h is well appointed for catering establishments, offering everything from pizzas to haute cuisine, together with specialty seafood restaurants.

How to get there: Follow the D788, the *Corniche Breton*, from Lannion by way of Perros-Guirec, or Trébeurden and Trégastel Plage. Parking space is available near the centre of the town, but be prepared to park elsewhere at the height of the holiday season.

Route description

There is no need for a formal route description to this walk. It can be varied at will and these instructions are therefore only to be used as a guide.

❶ From the town centre car park, walk down to the beach and turn right along the sea wall, then right again, uphill along a track signposted the *Sentier des Douaniers*. This track climbs past the entrances of several large houses, beneath the shade of occasional pine trees, then out towards the rock-strewn headland.

❷ Follow the coast, via the *Maison du Littoral* and the lifeboat station, bearing right with the curve of the coastline.

❸ At a tall granite cross, turn right along a narrow lane signposted the *Rue de Porz Rolland*. Go slightly uphill beneath huge pine trees bordering the gardens of large villas and then downhill along the road leading into the town centre and the car park.

Points of interest

Ⓐ The twelfth-century oratory of St Guirec stands above and to the left of the beach. St Guirec was the Celtic saint who introduced Christianity to the heathen peoples of this corner of Brittany. A stone statue of the saint has replaced an earlier wooden one. Local girls wanting to know what their marriage prospects were going to be, stuck needles into his nose: if the needle stayed put, a marriage was imminent! This custom was so popular that the head on the poor saint's statue simply collapsed through being prodded by so many needles. His present likeness is made of granite, so modern girls must use more reliable methods of seeking a husband.

Ⓑ The *Maison du Littoral*, field study centre, provides information about the rocks and wildlife of the surrounding coast. Call in for leaflets (in English as well as French and other languages). There is a numbered nature trail and you can also pick up a leaflet giving the fanciful names of the bewildering array of individual rocks. A visit to the information centre will also help to identify the birds seen on and around the rocks on the seaward side of the point. Cormorants, gannets, puffins and oyster catchers can be seen nearby, as well as more common varieties such as black-backed and herring gulls.

Ⓒ The lifeboat station is an ever-present reminder of the dangers of this treacherous coast. It is open to visitors, and photographs and graphic records give the history of rescues and earlier lifeboats stationed here on this rocky promontory.

Ⓓ The walk can be extended from Porz Rolland by following the *Sentier des Douaniers* footpath along the coast for a further three kilometres (two miles) to the Plage de Trestraou, and returning to Ploumanac'h by the local bus service or taxi cab.

Walk 12
ÎLE GRANDE

7 km (4 miles)   Easy

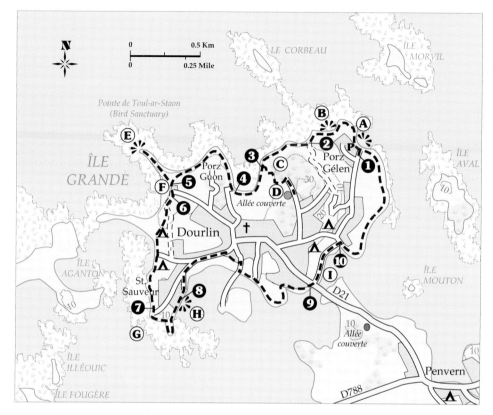

Island walking can be a most pleasurable activity; the sea is constantly in view, but with ever-changing aspects which alter around each twist and turn of the coastline. Navigation is simple, providing the island is not too big, because you always return to the starting point of the walk!

Île Grande is a low-lying island between Trégastel and Trébeurden on the *Côtes de Granit Rose*, the 'Pink Granite Coast'. A satisfying mixture of rocky coves, sandy beaches and pinewoods, it was once inhabited by an ancient Celtic tribe who have left their enigmatic message in the shape of two *allée couvertes*. One is in the centre of the island and the other near the bridge towards the tip of the narrow causeway leading from the mainland.

The bridge which links the island to the rest of Brittany is only short, but claims to cross the Atlantic Ocean! Narrow though the channel beneath the bridge may be, it is nevertheless filled by tidal water from the open sea.

The tour of the island starts near the sailing school at Porz Gélen and follows the coastline anticlockwise, never climbing more than a metre or two above the limits of the high tide mark.

Houses on the island are still the homes of fishermen, as Île Grande's other industry, quarrying, is in decline. At one time the island's rock was extensively quarried, following beds of the better grades deep into the ground, but now only small-scale working is carried out on the satellite island of Île Aganton to the west. For modern industry we must look to the east, on the mainland, to the radomes and space-age technology of Pleumeur Bodou.

There is a bar/restaurant next to the car park at the start of the walk and several other restaurants and cafés in the main village of Dourlin in the centre of the island.

How to get there: D65 from Lannion to Trébeurden and join the D788, *Corniche Breton,* to Penvern. Cross over to the island by the D21. Alternatively, follow the D21 all the way from Lannion via Pleumeur-Bodou.

Route description

❶ From the car park walk to the sailing school and turn left along a sandy path. Keep to the left of the harbour and then move out on to the sedge grass-covered shoreline.

❷ Keep to the right at the path junction, continuing to follow the coast.

❸ Turn left along a wide grassy path climbing gently inland. Walk almost to the highest point on the island to reach the *allée couverte.* Afterwards retrace your steps back to the coast and turn left to follow the coastline as before.

❹ Cross the sandy turning space at the end of the beach access track at Porz Guon. Bear right between the beach and a small pinewood, following the sandy path around a low grass and scrub-covered rocky point.

❺ Turn right and walk to the end of the rocky narrow point. Return and walk towards, then to the right of, the group of two-storied buildings of the field study complex.

❻ Away from the field study centre, follow a surfaced track until it begins to bear left. Leave it at this point to walk towards, then to the right of the camp site, following an indistinct path still bearing a little to the right, then ahead through sand dunes. Keep to the right of a boundary fence, and above the beach.

❼ Cross the harbour access and follow the grassy path around the sheltered bay. Bear right then go towards, then round a narrow gorse-covered headland. Turn left at the tip and begin to walk round a wide, shallow bay (muddy at low water), walking on the shore or above high water mark as dictated by the tide.

❽ Climb up to a road and turn right. Follow it and at the junction go to the right, around a small park, then right again to go down a narrow alleyway. Go forwards, then bear left along a narrow track on reaching the shoreline again. Walk along the edge of a salt marsh, following white/red waymarks until the island's main road is reached at the access bridge.

❾ Cross the main road and follow the side lane opposite, hugging the coast for about 350m (383yds).

❿ Where the shore road turns sharp left, go to the right along a track, past a row of houses, then follow the white/red waymarks forward on to a grassy path. Begin to bear left, working your way through sand dunes and to the left of the sandy shore of the shallow bay for about a kilometre (a little over half a mile), in order to reach the car park.

Points of interest

Ⓐ Viewpoint across the harbour where sailboarding enthusiasts show off their skills.

Ⓑ Viewpoint. The narrow island to the right is called *le Corbeau* (the crow), from the shape of the sharply piled beak-like rocks at its far end. The islet is joined to the main island at low water by a natural causeway of boulders and sand bars.

Ⓒ The partly-covered abandoned railway track is the sole relic of quarrying which was carried out on Île Grande. Stone was brought down from the centre of the island to vessels waiting off the rocky point on the right.

Ⓓ The *allée couverte* is a long, reasonably flat boulder supported on either side by a double row of smaller, upright, rocks. Sometimes *allées couvertes* are open to the four winds, but at other times they are covered by a mound of earth with a single entrance; this is one of the open variety. Built by a race of highly skilled people who, unfortunately, left us with no record of the purpose of their engineering feats. The most reasonable explanation is that it, like other forms of standing stones, had a religious meaning.

Ⓔ Viewpoint. Pointe de Toul-ar-Staon is a bird sanctuary. The nearby centre for ornithological studies is building up information on the local seabird population and occasionally cares for injured birds. The view from the point looks out on *la Manche* (the English Channel), or to the left into the Baie de Lannion.

Ⓕ Rock near the study centre was once quarried, leaving deep holes now filled with brackish water. The two closest to the centre usually have convalescing guillemots or other sea birds happily swimming on their still waters.

Ⓖ The harbour of St Sauveur offers safe anchorage for local and visiting craft.

Ⓗ The white radome peering above the skyline on the mainland is part of the Pleumeur-Bodou satellite telecommunications station. It played a vital part in early intercontinental TV transmissions and now handles world-wide telephone, TV and data-transmissions. The station is open to the public and there is also a museum of the history of long distance communications.

Ⓘ The little bridge crossing the 'Atlantic' leads to another *allée couverte.* Also further down the road, near the road junction at Penvern, a huge menhir, a standing stone, is 'converted' by roughly worked Christian symbols.

Walk 13
BEG LÉGUER

4 km (2.5 miles)   Moderate

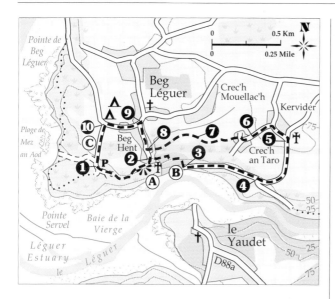

The village of Beg Léguer stands high above the northern tip of the Léguer estuary. The river, though navigable for small craft as far as Lannion, winds its way along a deeply-cut narrow valley, wooded for much of its length downstream from Lannion. Seawards, the Léguer valley and much of the surrounding countryside bears much comparison with the South Devon coastline.

Although the walk is short in distance, part of it follows a little-used path and has long interesting views. Winding its way through woodland and across green fields above the river, the walk makes an interesting evening stroll for anyone staying at the camp sites in Beg Léguer, or perhaps as a diversion while driving along the major arterial roads through this part of Brittany.

The approach along the north side of the Léguer estuary is from Lannion. The bustling market town of half-timbered and rose-red granite buildings lies at the junction of eight major routes. There has been some form of habitation around the river crossing since pre-historic times. Menhirs, standing stones, both untouched and 'Christianised', line the approaches to the town. An ancient port despite its difficult access to the open sea, Lannion's old quarter climbs the steep slopes to the north of the river. Interesting old buildings line streets surrounding the church in the centre of the town, but the best feature is the church at Brélévenez. Although only 400m (438yds) north of Lannion's town centre, but across a deeply-cut narrow side valley and reached by steep winding streets, Brélévenez is strictly a suburb of Lannion, and its church is the most important feature in the area.

Reached by 142 granite steps polished by the footsteps of countless devotees, climbing from the Rue de la Trinité, the church was built by the Knights Templar in the twelfth century, but has later additions. A semi-military body, the Knights Templar order was founded in 1118 to protect pilgrims from robbers while travelling to and from the Holy Land. Amassing great wealth, the knights founded banks based on 'temples' in Paris and London, but their arrogance towards national rulers led to their downfall. King Phillip of France, who was jealous of their wealth, plotted the order's downfall and it was suppressed in 1312.

There is one bar/alimentation (bar/general store), in Beg Léguer, but Lannion has a wider selection of bars, cafés, crêperies and restaurants.

How to get there: Direction of Lannion by D786 or D767 from the south, or D786 from Tréguier and D788 from Perros-Guirec; or the D65 from Trébeurden and D21 road from Île Grande in the north. A minor road high above the north side of the Léguer estuary leaves the D21 on the north-western outskirts of Lannion. Follow this road through Servel to reach Beg Léguer. Drive through the village and turn left at the signpost to the *Plage de Mez an Aod*. Go down the side road to its end and park in the open space on the left.

Route description

❶ Leave the car park and turn left to walk downhill along a track leading from the road end. Take the left fork in the narrowing track and walk downhill along a grassy footpath winding through scrubby trees and bushes. The path levels, then gradually climbs to a road end.

❷ At the road end, turn left and go towards the house on your right. Go past it and turn right along a path following its furthest boundary. Follow the path through trees, then begin to go steeply downhill, still under the shade of trees, towards the river estuary.

❸ At the small harbour, turn left and walk uphill along the access road.

❹ Bear left where a lane leaves the road. Follow the narrow country road around an uphill left-hand bend, gradually losing tree cover, but between steep earth and stone banks bordering open grassy fields.

❺ Look for a road junction marked by a stone village cross on your right. Turn left here, walk past an old farmhouse and a few cottages for 150m (164yds), then go left again at the next fork.

❻ Walk past several more cottages and on towards another fork, beside house number 24. Turn right and go past an old barn on the left. Pass a grassy mound and head towards, but not into, the farmyard directly ahead. Just beyond the mound, turn left along an indistinct field path beside an old boundary hedge. At first trees mark the boundary, but later it becomes submerged in wilder and scrubby undergrowth.

❼ At the end of the open field, more or less at the junction of the two overgrown boundaries, go forwards into the right-angle, through bushes for 2/3 metres. Step over two parallel wire fences, hopefully they will still be slack! Cross the next field and aim a little to the right of an oak tree marking its far boundary. Go forwards through scrubby bushes and a little downhill, into a meadow. Approaching farm buildings on the far side of the field, climb a rickety barrier blocking the field exit, and keeping to the right of the farm's outer walls, cross a small stream and start to bear right to climb up to a surfaced lane.

❽ Turn right and follow the narrow lane uphill towards the village.

❾ At the road junction, turn left and walk through Beg Léguer, past the bar/alimentation, following the road for about 340m (372yds).

❿ Turn left down the side road signposted to *Plage de Mez an Aod*, walking downhill past cottages and open fields to reach the car park.

Points of interest

Ⓐ Viewpoint. A venerable lichened calvary cross marks the view over the Léguer estuary where yachts and small inshore fishing boats are safely anchored below the village of le Yaudet. Mud flats, uncovered at low tide around the mouth of the river, are the haunt of wading birds, and are where the plaintive cries of oyster catchers can be heard long before their wheeling flight takes them to another part of the estuary.

Ⓑ Divert to the right to the tiny harbour for a rest, and watch the comings and goings of marine craft of all kinds.

Ⓒ The walk can be extended by following the access track on the right, down to the sheltered beach of Plage de Mez an Aod. Return by following the coastal path climbing steeply over Pointe Serval to enjoy the fine views across the estuary, or out towards the open sea.

Walk 14
ÎLE DE BATZ

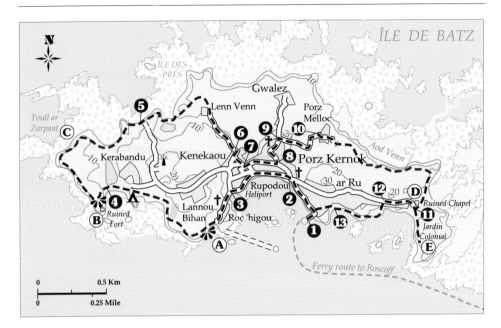

Brittany Ferries, en-route to and from Roscoff, pass close to the rocky Île de Batz. The 4km by 1km (2½ miles by ½ mile) island is only a kilometre (½ mile) offshore, across a narrow channel where jagged rocks are washed by the steep rise and fall of tidal waters.

The main feature of the Île de Batz is the 44m (144ft) high lighthouse in the middle of the island. Climbed by 200 steps, it has one of the finest views of the Brittany coast. Basically the home of fishermen, Île de Batz' mild climate allows early vegetables to be grown in the tiny fields sheltered by high stone and earth walls. Originally the island was a barren waste of rock and sand, but the rich soil has been created over the centuries from a mixture of seaweed and crushed shells. The *Jardin Colonial*, on the south-eastern tip of the island, has a collection of sub-tropical plants which thrive in the mild climate.

The island, whose name is pronounced 'Ba' by the locals, was converted to Christianity in the sixth century by a Welsh saint, St Paul. His name is shortened to St Pol in the Breton tongue and crops up in several places, such as St Pol-de-Leon to the south of Roscoff, where he became the first Bishop of Brittany.

St Pol is credited with having killed a fearsome dragon which lived in a cave on the western tip of Île de Batz, from where it terrorised the local fishermen. Setting out to trap it, the saint flung his cloak over the dragon's head and dragged the poor thing into the sea where it drowned. A ruined Romanesque chapel on the eastern tip of the island is built on the site of St Pol's original hermit's cell. What is reputed to be St Pol's cloak is in the island's church, and is thought to be oriental and dating from the eighth century. The island holds a *pardon* (a religious procession) on the Sunday closest to 26 July, when the ladies wear their traditional white-starched lace 'stove-pipe' hats and traditional Breton dresses. Music is provided by Breton bagpipes.

Roscoff is the home base for Brittany Ferries. The company was founded in the 1950s by the local farmers' co-operative who were looking for new markets for their vegetables. When they approached

Plymouth Chamber of Commerce, they are supposed to have been told that the city had no interest in dealing with Russia! Undeterred by Plymouth's alleged poor knowledge of the geography of western France, the farmers began shipping their vegetables to England. Aided by French government finance, what began as a scheme to transport cauliflowers, developed into today's major cross-channel ferry operation.

Visitors arriving at Roscoff by sea are usually intent on moving on as quickly as possible. This is a great pity as the old town is only a short distance away from the modern ferry terminal. The multi-tiered belfry tower of the church of Notre-Dame de Kroaz-Batz dominates the town. Inside it, a series of fine alabaster carvings are decorated with scenes from the Passion, and in keeping with the town's maritime traditions, ships and cannons. The latter are memorials to the *corsaires* (pirates), who preyed on English shipping in the sixteenth and seventeenth centuries, bringing wealth and prosperity to Roscoff.

For its size, Porz Kernok, Île de Batz' main village, has a wide range of restaurants and bars.

How to reach the Île de Batz:
D58 Morlais road, or the D10 from Plouescat to Roscoff. Ferries sail from the western side of the old port, taking 15 minutes to reach the island.

Route description

❶ From the ferry landing walk along the harbour wall and turn left to follow the shoreline street into the central square of Porz Kernok.

❷ Take the street furthest on the left, away from the church, and continue to walk round the sandy bay.

❸ At the heliport bear left to walk down the narrow lane, slightly inland from the sea. Beyond the last house, a footpath swings round the low headland and begins to follow the shoreline of a rocky bay. Head towards, and to the left of, a shallow reed-filled pond at the far side of the bay.

❹ Take the left fork, still following the coast, and walk to the seaward side of a complex of tiny fields. Go round the low headland, following the rocky shoreline.

❺ Continue ahead at the junction with a beach access track, onwards along the coast, past another pond then begin to bear right, inland. Follow the lane beginning at a small group of cottages and farm buildings and leading towards the main village of the island. Pass slightly larger fields and then a swampy area on your left.

❻ Follow the lane as it turns sharp right, then on towards the triangle of three lanes. Bear left here and into a more built-up area.

❼ Turn left at the T-junction and go through the main village.

❽ Turn left at the next T-junction, and move away from the village, out towards the fields again.

❾ At a junction marked by a calvary, turn right and follow the winding lane towards the group of cottages at Porz Melloc.

❿ Follow the narrowing track for a little way beyond the houses, then onwards where it becomes a path. Follow the sandy shoreline towards a low promontory, then go to the right around it and along a rocky foreshore.

⓫ Go to the left at the ruined chapel, towards the tropical garden. Return to the chapel and turn left to follow its access road around a small sandy bay.

⓬ Where a path leaves the road on the left, go down it to the beach and turn right, hugging the shoreline.

⓭ Do not go as far as the rocky headland overlooking the harbour, but climb up to the right from the beach and walk between the surrounding houses. The harbour access is to the left.

Points of interest

Ⓐ Viewpoint across the rocky channel. The graceful tracery of the church bell tower overlooks the oldest part of Roscoff.

Ⓑ Viewpoint. The ruins of an ancient fort make an attractive foreground to views of the Roscoff peninsula.

Ⓒ The rocky hollow of Toull ar Zarpant is reputed to be where St Pol killed the dragon.

Ⓓ The ruined chapel stands on the site of St Pol's cell, where Christianity first took root on the island.

Ⓔ Jardin Colonial. Semi-tropical and other delicate plants flourish in the rich soil of this corner of the island, enjoying its mild frost-free climate.

Walk 15
BOURG-BLANC

6 km (4 miles)   Easy

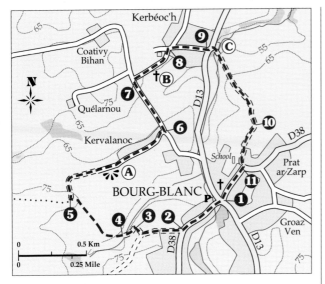

The walk described here is a complete change from the others in this guide and offers the chance to explore a small provincial town well off the usual tourist routes. It starts next to Bourg-Blanc's attractively modern town hall, the *Mairie*, contrasting the stately old church which stands on the opposite side of the road, above a high stone wall. Field tracks and traffic-free lanes wind round the sleepy provincial town.

Over the past decade or so, walking has become a popular form of exercise in France, almost rivalling Britain. The paths and tracks of this walk are used by locals on their evening or afternoon strolls around the town, or as part of a longer tour of the district.

Being a small town away from the main tourist routes, Bourg-Blanc only has one or two bars, but there are boulangeries and other shops where food can be bought.

How to get there: Bourg-Blanc is on the D13, roughly half way between Brest and Plougernau. Park in front of the *Mairie*, or in quiet side streets on either side of the church.

Route description

❶ Follow the side street opposite the church, signposted to Milizac and St Renan.

❷ Where the road begins to bear left at the end of a row of older houses, turn right along an unsurfaced farm track, waymarked by double yellow stripes. Follow this track below, and to the right, of modern houses, out into the open fields. Take the right fork at a track junction and walk gently downhill between banks of wild flowers. Ignore turnings into fields on either side.

❸ Keep to the main track which swings left, then right, across a low-lying swampy area drained by a small stream.

❹ Continue ahead, along what has now become a path between fields.

❺ Turn right along the partly surfaced lane, through the farm hamlet of Kervalanoc, to the lane end at a T-junction.

❻ Go to the left at the junction. Follow the surfaced road across a broad valley lined with rich farmland.

❼ Turn right at the crossroads and go past the small chapel on your right.

❽ Bear right at the staggered crossroads by a farmhouse, go downhill past a group of modern houses.

❾ Cross the busy D13 with care and follow the wide unsurfaced track on the right of the tall roadside building.

❿ The track improves on its approach to the outskirts of Bourg-Blanc. Bear left with it next to the school.

⓫ Turn right on entering the street to go downhill past the church. The *Mairie* is on the right of the crossroads.

Points of interest

Ⓐ Viewpoint. The distant view of Finistère's rolling farmland with the distinctive spire of Bourg-Blanc's church in the middle distance.

Ⓑ St Urfold's Chapel. The Celtic missionary who first planted his cross at this place probably did so on the site of an even older religion. Round arched doorways suggest that the church dates from at least the eleventh century, but surprisingly the date on the venerable looking preaching cross in the churchyard is only 1927.

Ⓒ The tall building beside the main road is now a private house, but was once the local corn mill. The mill-race flows strongly beneath the bridge at its side.

Walk 16
POINTE DE DINAN

4 km (2.5 miles)   Easy

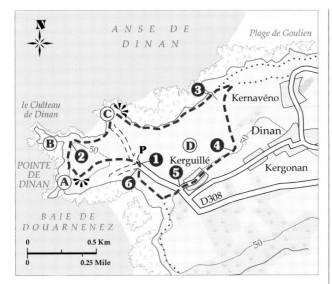

the right uphill on a faint grassy path through gorse and heather. The path improves as it climbs.

4 Turn right on joining a wide grassy path. Follow it into the hamlet of Kerguillé. Walk past the double row of cottages and small farms, following a narrow winding lane, slightly downhill.

5 Cross the road and follow the partly overgrown sunken concrete path, between gorse bushes, down towards the beach.

6 Turn right on reaching the sandy beach access track, following it uphill and back to the car park.

Points of interest

A Viewpoint. Looking south across the Baie de Douarnenez to the Pointe du Raz.

B The *Château de Dinan* is aptly named. The group of rocks on the opposite side of the natural limestone arch could easily be mistaken for a ruined castle. The surrounding cliffs are used by rock climbers, but do not attempt to use their exposed access path across the 'bridge'. Worn limestone can be very slippery, and also the slopes on either side of it are covered in loose pebbles. **The path is unprotected and can be very dangerous, especially during wet or windy weather.**

C Viewpoint. Overlooking the wide silvery strand of the Plage de Kerziguenou. The nearest access to it is from a narrow road below the tiny village of Goulien, which has a corner of the long beach named entirely to itself.

D Keguillé village. As with many communities in areas of poor farmland, some of the cottages, once the homes of farm workers, are now holiday homes. One or two elderly farmers still hang on to their traditional livelihoods.

The Crozon peninsula is famous for its dramatic sea cliffs. Some of the finest and most spectacular rock scenery can be found around the high crags bordering the Pointe de Dinan. A well-maintained path, once part of the coastguard's patrol track, follows a safe route around the tops of the awesome cliffs, never more than 500 metres (547yds), from the car park.

This short walk links a series of dramatic viewpoints and need only take an hour or so while visiting the nearby resort of Crozon. The town itself makes an ideal base for exploring the sea cliffs around the peninsula, both on foot or by boat. Crozon itself stands inland, well back from its twin, crescent-moon shaped beaches. Its church is its main on-shore feature; the altarpiece has over 400 exquisitely painted wooden figures representing the martyrdom of the Theban Legion in Armenia.

The nearest cafés, bars and restaurants are in Crozon which is about six kilometres (4 miles) to the east of Pointe de Dinan.

How to get there: D887 west along the Presqu'île de Crozon from the N165-E60 Brest to Quimper road, via Châteaulin, to Crozon. The D308 west from Crozon is signposted to the Pointe de Dinan. Car parking space is at the road end.

Route description

1 From the car park walk uphill and go to the left, and then right, along the top of the exposed limestone cliffs.

2 Bear right away from the castelated rocks of the *Château de Dinan*, then left and right again, following the cliff path around the next headland.

3 Cross a little stream and climb the slight rise opposite, then go to

Walk 17
THE CHAPEL OF ST SAMSON   4 km (2.5miles)   Easy

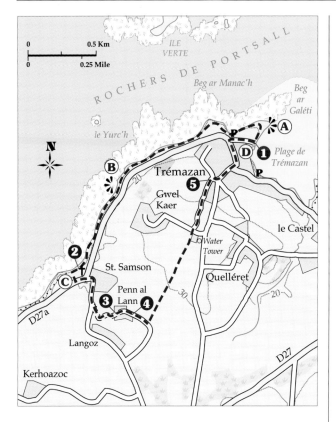

The coast between the seaside resorts of Portsall and Porspoder is low and rocky, with narrow sandy bays and coves sheltered from the wind. Above one of these coves stands a lonely memorial to the efforts of St Samson, an early Celtic missionary who brought Christianity to this part of Finistère. Inland are snug farmhouses and villages huddled behind the meagre shelter offered by the low rolling countryside. Fields are small and guarded by solid walls of stone and turf, but with the frost-free climate local farmers manage to grow crops much earlier than those inland.

Porspoder is to the south, a pleasant looking village which sprawls languidly on either side of its church. It is where St Budoc, another Celtic saint who later became the Bishop of Dol-de-Bretagne, landed. Portsall's bay marks the northern point of the walk. The little fishing village relies on catching crabs and lobsters, fruits of the sea that can be enjoyed in its quayside restaurants.

Trémazan, from where the walk starts, is on the opposite side of the bay from Portsall. Its anchorage is more exposed than

Portsall's, but it has the better beach. Nearby are the ruins of Trémazan Castle which is linked to the romantic story of Tristan and Iseult. Tanguy du Châtel was born at Trémazan Castle. By murdering the Duke of Burgundy while the latter was negotiating with the French Dauphin in an attempt to end the Hundred Years' War, he prolonged the conflict. This reckless act was probably one of the causes of England's loss of its lands in France.

The walk follows the line of sea cliff as far as St Samson's chapel, before turning inland, along quiet lanes and trackways back to Trémazan.

Portsall has excellent restaurants specialising in fish dishes, and also a crêperie and a selection of bars.

How to get there: D26 direct from Brest, or the D68 to Porspoder and the D27a coastal road north-east. Park overlooking the rocks of Beg ar Manac'h, or in the direction of Portsall next to the Plage de Trémazan.

Route description
❶ Follow the coast path on the west side of the sandy bay, around the low headland of Beg ar Gaiéti and the rocks of Beg ar Manac'h. Continue along the clifftop path, parallel to the road. Keep to the path until you reach St Samson's clifftop chapel.
❷ Turn left at the chapel, away from the coast and cross the road. Walk up the side lane opposite, bearing right at a turning below a group of houses. Go forwards for another 250m (273yds), then fork left on to an unsurfaced track

leading towards a group of farm buildings.

❸ Go through the farmyard at Penn al Lann and out along its access drive past a large modern house surrounded by a hedge of tall pines.

❹ About a hundred metres beyond the large house, the roadway makes a sharp right-hand turn. Go to the left here, along a grassy cart track between the shelter of tall hedges. Head towards the tall water tower topped by a navigation light and make for a group of cottages on its left. Continue forwards from the cottages, along a narrow road, heading back towards Trémazan.

❺ On entering the oldest part of Trémazan, turn right and walk through the village, past low stone farmhouses and white-washed cottages. Turn left at the stepped village cross and go down a narrow lane, then turn left on reaching the coast road. Follow it into the village square then bear right, and left again. The car park of Beg ar Manac'h is through the village, to the right where the road turns left following the coastline. If you have parked near the beach, turn right on joining the coast road when entering Trémazan.

Points of interest

Ⓐ Viewpoint. Across the sands of the Plage de Trémazan to the harbour of Portsall with its colourful array of anchored boats.

Ⓑ Viewpoint. Looking to the left along the coast towards the rocky Pointe de Landunvez. Beyond the point is the red-topped light of Le Four Phare, guiding coastal shipping in and out of the busy port of Brest.

Atlantic swell breaking over the rocky foreshore is an ever-present reminder of the power of the sea.

On 16 March 1978, the *Amoco Cadiz* went aground on Men Goulven in the outermost rocks guarding Portsall Bay. The disastrous effect of the subsequent oil spillage on marine life and to the local economy can only be imagined and took years to overcome. The accident is commemorated by one of the massive anchors from the *Amoco Cadiz*, which is now sited above Portsall's harbour wall.

Ⓒ St Samson's Chapel. Having crossed the open sea from Wales in nothing more than a leather coracle, the Celtic missionary converted the local population, preaching from beside a simple stone cross. The chapel stands on the simple cell where St Samson lived.

Ⓓ Look out for the ancient stone cross set into the wall of the last house on the right when approaching the car park above Beg ar Manac'h.

Walk 18
POINTE DE CORSEN

6 km (4 miles)   Moderate

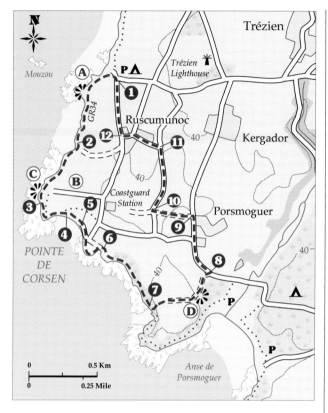

Ruscumunoc. Brest can be reached from the channel ports of St Malo and Roscoff via the N12-E50.

Route description

❶ Go down towards the beach and turn left. Climb the grassy coastal path where clusters of pink thrift vie for attention with views of the open sea and sandy bays. Follow white/red striped waymarks of the GR 34 long distance path along the sea cliff.

❷ Keeping to the right at the junction with an access track, continue to follow the path along the clifftop.

❸ Go to the left, away from the Pointe de Corsen, following a springy turf path high above a sandy bay.

❹ Bear right at the path junction, then right again on joining the beach access road.

❺ Follow the narrow road until it begins to turn left, then go to the right along a path marked by slender posts waymarked with double yellow stripes as well as the white/red GR waymarks. Follow the path around a small rocky headland.

❻ Bear right, then left, on to a rough track and right again, above a series of rocky coves.

❼ Where the path crosses the top of a deeply cut cove, turn sharp left and leave the cliff path. Walk uphill for a little way to join a field track. Keeping roughly parallel to the sandy bay below and on your right, walk over the brow of the slight rise in front. Go forwards and downhill to the Porsmoguer road.

❽ Turn left on reaching the road. Follow it uphill by walking along its grassy verge. Go past the turning for the Pointe de

This walk is along windswept clifftops, high above tempting, but frequently inaccessible, golden sandy coves, and leads to the most westerly point on the French mainland. A turquoise sea washes the base of cliffs where scuba divers explore the clear depths, searching the dark recesses between rocks for hiding lobsters.

Starting at sea level beside an uncluttered sandy beach, the path climbs steadily along the open clifftop, heading towards the Pointe de Corsen. From there it makes for the wide bathing beach of the Anse de Porsmoguer, before turning inland for the lush fertile lands of prosperous farms sheltering in the lee of the point.

There is only one source of refreshment convenient to this walk, the crêperie situated above the beach at Ruscumunoc and close to the car park. However, Lampaul-Plouarzel, which is a little to the north along the coast by an unclassified country road, has a better range of restaurants.

How to get there: D5 north-west from Brest to Lampaul-Plouarzel, then minor road south-west past the lighthouse at Trézien to

Corsen Coastguard Station, onwards towards a large house on the right at the top of the hill.

9 On the brow of the hill, turn left and follow a grassy field track. Aim towards a group of tall pines, ahead and to the right of the coastguard station.

10 Turn right on reaching the pine trees and walk along the by-road pointing in the direction of the Trézien lighthouse.

11 Go to the left along a lane, past a riding school, and take the next left fork beside an old asbestos roofed farmhouse.

12 Turn right at the T-junction. Go downhill past the crêperie to your left and join the beach access road. The car park is directly opposite.

Points of interest

A Viewpoint from the small headland, towards the group of offshore islands, the Île d'Ouessant. The archipelago of tiny windswept islands and rocks is part of the Amorique Nature Park. Similar to a National Park in England and Wales, the site is protected against exploitation by developers. Wildlife is also preserved, and sea birds nest on the rocky islets and cliffs. It takes an hour by ferry to reach Île d'Ouessant from le Conquet, the nearest port to Pointe de Corsen, or around two hours from Brest. The windswept island which only measures 7km by 4km (4 by 2½ miles), and where traditionally it is the woman who proposes marriage, can be explored by bicycles hired near the landing stage at Lampaul, the main village.

From this clifftop viewpoint, side paths radiate down to tempting sandy coves; but take care not to be on the wrong side of a headland against the rapidly incoming tide. **Do not on any account attempt to walk by linking coves. Not all of them have an access path, and the cliffs are unsafe.**

B The radio mast and large building on the left is a coastguard station monitoring coastal shipping in and out of the busy port of Brest.

C Pointe de Corsen. This is the most westerly part of Finistère and also of the French mainland. When the Romans conquered this part of Gaul, as France was then called, they named this the then limit of their empire *finis terre*, literally 'Land's End'. Finistère is the modern version of the Latin title.

The point marks the joining of the Atlantic Ocean and the English Channel (*la Manche*). An orientation plaque indicates important features along the coast and names the outer islands visible from this point. Humorously, a signpost points west to New York and east to Paris and Moscow. A more serious note though, is struck by the large stone commemorating local sailors lost at sea, and a smaller rock gives details of some of the more notable events along the coast.

D Viewpoint. Overlooking the white sandy bay of the Anse de Porsmoguer, a perfect place for a swim on a sunny day.

The English have not always been welcome visitors to Porsmoguer. In June 1512, a raiding party of English privateers which had earlier landed at le Conquet, set fire to the Manoir de Porsmoguer a little way above the beach. You can see the site of the building as you climb the road between route description pointer numbers **8** and **9**. The manor is long gone, but a farmhouse now marks the site.

Walk 19
POINTE DE ST MATHIEU

4 km (2.5 miles)   Moderate

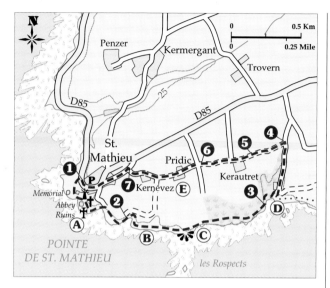

A tall white lighthouse with a red top stands high above the sea-washed cliffs of St Mathieu's point. Set amidst the ruins of a Benedictine monastery, it marks the turning point for shipping heading towards the busy port of Brest.

Pointe de St Mathieu is at the southern tip of a blunt peninsula jutting out into the Atlantic beyond Brest. The fishing harbour and holiday beaches of le Conquet lie to the north along a rugged coast of rocky coves and exposed bays.

The walk can be combined with a visit to le Conquet. The village sits at the mouth of an *aber*, or estuary, its harbour protected against storms by the fish-hook shaped Pointe de Kermorvan. During the time of the Napoleonic wars, no doubt remembering the sacking of the district by English privateers in 1512 (see Walk 17 — Pointe de Corsen), a series of forts was built along this part of the coast, starting opposite le Conquet. The town is one of the oldest fishing ports in Finistère and its history can be traced in the Sea Museum near the church. Both the museum and the church, together with the surrounding houses of the oldest part of the town, are set back a little way above the promenade.

Plougonvelin is to the east of the Pointe de St Mathieu, along the coast leading to Brest. A pleasant holiday resort with a sheltered wide sandy beach, the town is enhanced by the delightful practice of painting brightly-coloured murals on the gable ends of buildings surrounding its traffic-free town centre.

The short walk described here starts beside the lighthouse. It then follows a clifftop path around the Pointe de St Mathieu, before moving inland along a farm lane winding between sheltering field

boundaries, back to the car park.

N.B. There are one or two short, but steep, inclines where the path crosses, or avoids side gullies. The path is well maintained and safe, but the steep sections can be slippery after rain.

The abbey restaurant is next to the car park and is highly recommended. Nearby le Conquet has a wider selection of small restaurants specialising in crab and lobster dishes.

How to get there: D789 le Conquet road, west from Brest, then via Plougonvelin and the D85 to the Pointe St Mathieu. Car parking is next to the abbey entrance, or beside the coast road heading towards le Conquet.

Route description

❶ From the abbey car park, walk towards the sailors' memorial and the impotently rusting guns left over from World War 2. Turn left above the jagged rocks of the point and follow the path, past the coastguard station and beneath the white and red lighthouse. Go past the ruined outer walls of the abbey and bear right away from a tiny chapel, then begin to go left at an old stone cross. Follow the grassy path along the open clifftop.

❷ Keep to the right at a track junction and follow the clifftop path, through scrubby bushes, then forwards, still keeping to the scrub-covered clifftop, winding in and out as dictated by the line of the coast.

❸ Go steeply downhill into a deep little side valley. Cross it and climb the opposite side, then aim to the right of a cottage. Go past it and then past the house next door which has three dormer windows. Turn left at the house to walk up the steep, narrow and tree-lined access lane.

❹ Turn left on to a rough field track and walk towards the farm buildings ahead.

❺ Go to the right of the farmhouse, and where a surfaced lane bears to the right away from the farm, continue ahead along a field track.

❻ Cross an access road and follow the surfaced road opposite, towards, then between farm buildings on the left and a large house to the right. Walk on by a cart track, bearing right at a junction to reach the next farm. Go through its yard and out along the surfaced access drive.

❼ Go to the left at the junction, away from the main road, and follow the lane towards the abbey entrance and car park.

Points of interest

Ⓐ Pointe de St Mathieu. The storm-wracked ruins of the monastery are well worth exploring, as is the small exposition. A Benedictine order, the monastery was founded by St Tanguy in the sixth century. The reason the monastery is named after St Matthew, instead of its founder, is linked to a rather curious tale. When the head of the Apostle St Matthew was brought to Europe from Ethiopia, the ship carrying it was caught in a violent storm off the Finistère coast. Fearing for their lives, the sailors held the saint's head aloft in supplication, and miraculously a calm channel appeared, leading them safely into harbour. By the time of the French Revolution, the monastery had built up tremendous power and wealth from its land ownings and fishing interests. Demanding change, the 'New Order' confiscated all the wealth and trappings, turning the monks out into the world. The abbey buildings were abandoned and its stonework became a ready source of building material for the surrounding area.

The lighthouse is usually open to visitors who must climb its winding staircase if they are to enjoy the vast panorama of the Finistère coast. The view ranges from the Pointe du Raz in the south, to the Ushant islands far out to sea to the west. To the left, and set back in the centre of the huge bay leading to Brest, is the oddly-shaped Crozon Peninsula and its sunny beaches. The peninsula and the Ushants are part of the Parc Naturel Régional d'Armorique, a huge complex of both off-shore, coastal and inland areas of environmentally protected sites.

A poignant memorial to all the French sailors who died in the 1914-18 war stands on the tip of the headland of the Pointe de St Mathieu. Close to it are the rusting guns set up during the 1939-45 war, part of Hitler's Atlantic Wall, in the vain hope of repelling Allied invasion.

Ⓑ The path was originally made to allow coastguard's access to remote landing places along the coast. The coastguard's work was two-fold, in that they had to keep a look-out for smugglers and also help save the lives of sailors shipwrecked on this exposed coast.

Ⓒ Viewpoint. Ships of all shapes and sizes pass to and fro beneath the point, on their way in and out of Brest.

Ⓓ The slender tall white marker post beside the path is complemented by another further along the coast to the east. The distance between them is used by shipping to calibrate their speed.

Ⓔ Looking like something out of a fairy tale, the small ivy-covered château at Pridic is in fact a working farm.

Walk 20
POINTE DES ESPAGNOLS.

7 km (4 miles) Easy

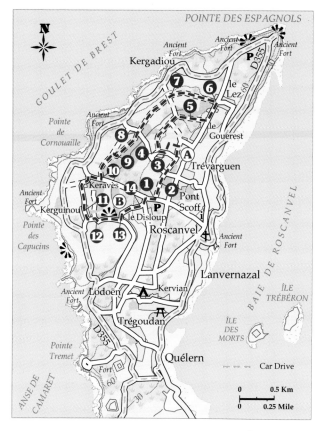

The Pointe des Espagnols is the northernmost of a series of horn-like projections which stick out from the Presqu'île de Crozon. The 'almost island' divides the Baie de Douarnenez, creating a huge area of deep sheltered water around the port of Brest.

In 1590 Philip II of Spain decided that Brittany would be an ideal addition to his empire and sent an invasion fleet to capture Brest. Rather than make a frontal attack on the port, the Spaniards captured the northern tip of the Crozon peninsula, directly opposite Brest. Here they stayed for over four years, not moving, but resisting attempts to dislodge them. In 1594, Queen Elizabeth I of England, becoming worried about another Spanish Armada, sent 2000 soldiers to help the French dislodge their unwelcome neighbours. Ever since then the promontory has been known as the *Pointe des Espagnols*.

The Spanish were not the only nation to have covetous ideas towards this part of the Brittany coast. Following an annoying stream of invaders, in 1689 the Crozon peninsula was heavily fortified. These defences were successfully tested in 1694 when an Anglo-Dutch invasion was repelled. The few men who reached the shore after their ships were sunk by the coastal batteries, were put to flight by the Breton militia, a kind of home guard armed with pitchforks and other farm implements.

During the Napoleonic wars, the brilliant military architect Sébastien Le Pestre de Vaubin, built a series of massive forts, turning the Pointe des Espagnols peninsula into one vast impenetrable stronghold. Now mainly overgrown, the massive fortifications speak eloquently of their one-time strength.

Even though parts of the old fortresses are still used by the French army, the rest are accessible from the D355 which follows the coastline around the tip of the Pointe des Espagnols.

To appreciate the peninsula more fully, this walk is best combined with a short car drive, starting at the Château Vaubin in Camaret-sur-Mer. The massive castle, one of Vaubin's masterpieces, is on the tip of the harbour wall overlooking the anchorage and sandy bay. Inside the castle a museum charts the history of the area and the works of Vaubin. Nearby is the chapel of Notre-Dame-de-Rocamadour, where shipwrecked sailors have donated model ships commemorating their often miraculous escapes.

Following Camaret's seafront, the road then turns inland a

44

little way to meet the D355. This road hugs the coast and heads north towards the fortified headland. Reaching the narrowest part, it passes through a series of defensive walls by massive gateways, then bears right to climb to a road junction. Take the left fork here and drive round the coast, stopping as your fancy takes, and visit the ancient earthworks and abandoned batteries of the one-time fortress.

There are many viewpoints, especially at the Pointe des Espagnols itself. Park a little to the west of the point and walk down the side road on the left, through a battlemented wall and down to the viewpoint overlooking shipping lanes in and out of Brest.

The walk itself is along by-lanes and trackways, through natural woodland, over moorland and past slumbering hamlets, with views of activity around naval bases in the Baie de Roscanvel. Roscanvel has a friendly hotel/retaurant and a boulangerie, and there is a crêperie at the hamlet of Keravès near point **10** on the walk.

How to get there: For the walk, drive on into Roscanvel and bear right above its tiny harbour, as far as the church. Turn right at the church, then take the first left along a side road climbing to the scattered hamlet of le Disloup. About 80 metres (88yds) beyond a concrete water tank, park on the grassy verge near the corner of the side track on the right, called *Chemin du Menez Brug*.

Route description

1 Follow the unsurfaced track to the right of the road leading between moorland and scrub, towards a tall pinewood. Ignore any side tracks.

2 Go through the pinewood, and in sight of two cottages, turn left on to a path across a meadow. Follow the right-hand boundary hedge to the opposite end of the field, then turn left on a grassy cart track until you reach a by-road.

3 Turn right at the road and follow it past a group of old cottages and farm buildings.

4 Where the road bears left beside the last cottage, turn right and follow a track across open fields, then bear left when it reaches an area of scrubland. Ignore any side tracks.

5 At the top of a slight rise, go past a bungalow and turn left on to a minor road. Follow the road for 250m (274yds), past a farm cottage on the left, then a modern house on your right.

6 Turn left at a cross roads opposite a surfaced lane called *Hameau du Lez*. Follow the rough unsurfaced track on the left, slightly downhill into scrub woodland.

7 Follow the track ahead at a crossing, through scrub and gorse.

8 Cross a minor road and continue ahead along the track.

9 Turn sharp right with the track, then left at the track junction. Walk down the track until it joins a road.

10 Turn right at the road. Follow it to a junction and go to the left, then bear right and left again, around the crêperie at Keravès. Walk on towards, then through the next hamlet, called Kerguinou.

11 Through Kerguinou turn left down a roughly surfaced lane for about 150m (164yds) and turn right at the fork.

12 From the fork, follow the lane uphill through mixed natural woodland and between banks of wild flowers.

13 Take the left fork at the junction with another lane. Follow it round a sharp right-hand bend, beginning to go gently uphill in order to join a by-road.

14 Turn left at the by-road, then right at the junction with another road. Follow this uphill and back to the car.

Points of interest

A A grassy mound on the left marks the site of an old mine. The region is famous for its crystalline forms of quartz. Many fine examples of these and other semi-precious stones can be seen in the Maison des Minéraux at St Hernot (see Walk 21).

B Viewpoint. The unspoilt woodland is a paradise of wild flowers. Sun-loving plants such as ragged robin, cornflower and red campion bloom along the sides of the lane, and in the shadier recesses beneath the branches of trees, shade-tolerant herb Paris thrives quite happily. Free from the deadly effects of insecticides, iridescent dragonflies and butterflies of all shapes and sizes wing their way from plant to plant.

Walk 21
CAP DE LA CHÈVRE

6 km (4 miles)   Moderate/Strenuous

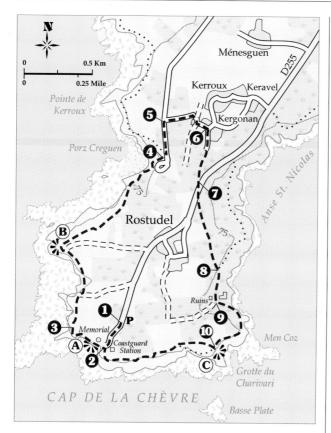

Presqu'île de Crozon. **N.B. As there are several quite steep sections on this walk, it is not suitable in wet weather, especially near route description pointers ❸, ❽, ❾ and ❿.** Strong-soled shoes are highly recommended and children should be told not to run, or go too close to the cliff edge.

The nearest places for refreshment are the nearby holiday resort of Morgat and its neighbour Crozon. Both places have a wide range of high standard restaurants and bars, as well as a number of good shops.

How to get there: As for Walk 16, to Crozon, then continue by the D887 to Morgat. Turn right in the town centre, away from the promenade, and follow the the D255 through St Hernot to the road-end car park near the coastguard station at Cap de la Chèvre.

Route description

❶ From the car park go past the traffic barrier and walk towards the coastguard station.

❷ Go to the right on reaching the coastguard station, past a tall beacon and the memorial. Keeping to the left of open fields, move out on to a path along the grassy clifftop.

❸ Keeping well back from the cliff edge, follow the well maintained cliff path. Go past a side access track joining from your right, then go steeply down into a dry gully. Cross the dry gully bottom and climb its opposite side, then follow the path around the next exposed headland. Beyond the headland the path follows a more even course on the left of a rolling open hillside. On reaching scrubland, the path

You are not likely to meet any goats along the path around the *Cap de la Chèvre*, but a reasonable head for heights and steady feet will be necessary on this walk.

The cape marks the southern tip of the Crozon peninsula. High limestone cliffs jut out into the stormy waters of the Atlantic, one of the most exposed parts of the Finistère coastline. The path is well established as it was once part of the *Sentier Côtier*, the old route patrolled by coast watchers in the days before radar and other scientific aids.

Being made from limestone, the cliffs are riddled with caves and sea-washed grottos. None are accessible from the clifftop path, but there are regular sailings (weather permitting) from nearby Morgat.

Morgat faces a wide sandy bay the Anse de Morgat, and makes an excellent holiday centre, either for a lazy seaside break, or as a base for exploring the southern tip of the Crozon peninsula, the

46

zig-zags down the slope towards, then into a steep rock and grass-filled gully. Follow the gully, almost to sea level, before climbing to the right and out of it by further zig-zags. At the clifftop join an access lane a little to the left of a car turning point.

❹ Turn left on joining the lane and walk along it to a junction with another lane.

❺ Go to the right at the junction, along the lane which leads towards a group of farm buildings. At the farm, go to the right to join a cart track into the farmyard. Directly opposite the farmhouse, turn left along a narrow walled lane, heading towards a scattered group of cottages.

❻ Turn right at the T-junction, go past a row of cottages, then out along a narrow grassy field track, heading towards an open moor.

❼ Cross the main road, diagonally right, to follow a track through yellow flowering gorse bushes and over rough heather moorland. Follow this track down towards the coast.

❽ Join a side track and turn half-right across the scrub-covered steep hillside, high above the sea. Go downhill towards a group of ruined buildings.

❾ Ignore a track going to the right and away from the ruins.

Turn sharp left along the bush-covered slope, heading towards the exposed upper limits of a line of limestone sea cliffs. Follow the top of the rocky cliffs, then bear right to climb the open hillside and begin to go round the next headland.

❿ Take the right-hand path, away from the clifftop. Make for the edge of a small wood of wind-stunted trees. Bear left along the woodland edge, back towards the sea cliffs. Follow the path, bearing right high above the sea, all the way to the coastguard station. Turn right and go past the white coastguard look-out post to reach the car park.

Points of interest

Ⓐ Viewpoint. Looking out into the open waters of the Baie de Douarnenez. To the south is the long peninsula of the Pointe du Raz and the windswept Île de Sein. One of the strongest currents along the Finistère coast flows between the island and the Pointe du Raz, and it is where many proud ships have been sunk. The imposing Memorial Atlantique commemorates the all too numerous maritime disasters.

Ⓑ Viewpoint. The unnamed headland not only makes a natural stopping place for a rest after the steep climb out of the narrow gully to its east, but also it offers a delightful vantage point to watch sea birds gliding on up-draughts along the coast. Tankers following a coast-hugging route must plot a careful course between the outer skerries and islands, if they are to keep within the bounds of safety.

Ⓒ Viewpoint. Due south is the Pointe du Raz and below the clifftop is the Grotte du Charivari. The limestone coast is riddled with caves such as the one below this point. Being at the foot of sheer cliffs, none of the caves near the Cap de la Chèvre are accessible from the land. However, one group is visited regularly by pleasure boats sailing from Morgat, the pretty holiday resort a little way along the coast. Known as l'Autel (the Altar), the sea cave which measures 15m (49ft) high by 80m (262ft) deep, has, when the combination of tide and sun are right, a wonderful array of colourful effects. There is also a smaller group of caverns between Morgat and le Portzic known as les Petites Grottes, which can be reached along the beach at low tide.

Colourful minerals and crystals found in the area are on display in the Musée Minéralogique at St Hernot, about half way along the road between Cap de la Chèvre and Morgat.

Walk 22
MÉNEZ-MIKEL

5 km (3 miles)   Moderate

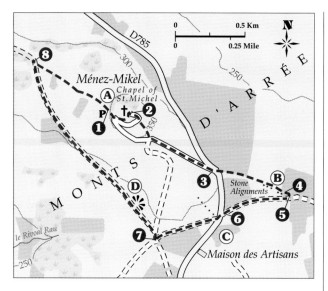

How to get there: D785 south from Morlaix, or north from Pleyben. Pleyben is linked to the central Finistère coast by way of the N164 and N165/E60. Turn off the D785 at the signposted turning for Chapelle de St Michel. Park below the summit.

Route description

❶ From the car park climb the flight of wooden steps leading from it to the hilltop Chapel of St Michel.

❷ Face the direction of the reservoir and go down the private road away from the summit. Where this road veers to the right, take the flight of steps on the left and go down to the access road. Turn left and walk down the road to reach the main road.

❸ Cross the road, with care, and go towards a break in the dense pine forest opposite.   Follow a rough path, gently downhill along a fire break, then out on to the boggy open moor. Look for the line of ancient stones, partly hidden in the heather, and follow them towards another section of pine forest.

❹ An indistinct path beside the aligned stones leads to an earth banked ditch. Cross the ditch and turn immediately right, following it towards a line of pine trees. On reaching the trees, re-cross the ditch, and bear left more or less beside the ditch and into the trees. Go to the right as dictated by the path, veering away from the densest woodland.

❺ Cross a muddy side ditch and join a forest track. Turn right and follow it through the mature pine forest.

❻ Re-cross the main road and

Inland from Finistère's rugged coastline, and in the heart of Brittany, lie a range of low rocky moors known as the Monts d'Arrée. Barely reaching 390 metres (1280ft), the moors are dotted with strange outcrops and saw-toothed pinnacles of weather-worn granite, which despite their low altitude still manage to give a mountainous feel to the area. Lonely winding valleys, shunned by major roads, lead to remote villages of quaint stone cottages and unspoilt old farmhouses. The whole region is part of the Parc Naturel Régional d'Armorique which stretches from the off-shore islands beyond the Crozon peninsula, north-eastwards almost to the ancient town of Morlaix. The mixed region of forest, moorland and marine environments is now protected from development within this regional park.

The chapel of St Michel de Brasparts stands on an exposed hilltop to the west of the D785, Pleyben to Morlaix road. This hillock, Ménez-Mikel, is typical of the exposed summits of the Monts d'Arrée, but is the only one revered as a religious site. Starting at the chapel, the walk follows the line of a track which has probably been in use since pre-historic times, out over partly-forested moors; then close to a busy road for a stretch.

There is a café attached to the Maison des Artisans craft centre which is at the side of the road from the south, prior to the turning for Ménez-Mikel. Further down the road in Brasparts, small rural bars and family-run crêperies and restaurants offer simple, but well-prepared food. There are also one or two food shops in the village selling the basic supplies for picnics.

follow the wide stoney track opposite. Ignore a path going to the right and waymarked by a horseshoe sign. Climb steadily uphill along the right-hand edge of a pine forest.

7 At the junction of five tracks, take the second on your right (ignore the first, a signposted path pointing to Mt St Michel). Follow a rough gravel-surfaced path, gently climbing the rough open moor. Aim for a clump of trees on the skyline, below and to the left of the summit of Ménez-Mikel.

8 Turn right at the track junction and follow the wide rough-surfaced path, along the moorland ridgetop, towards the cone-like mountain of Ménez-Mikel, and so back to the car park.

Points of interest

(A) The Chapel of St Michel de Brasparts stands at 381m (1250ft) on the summit of Ménez-Mikel, marking the southern end of the Ménez-Kador ridge, in the Monts d'Arrée. The simple chapel was built in the seventeenth century on the site of what is considered to be the temple of the pagan Celtic sun-god Bénélos. Local folk legend speaks of a struggle between followers of the older religion and the missionaries who brought Christianity to this remote corner of Brittany. Masses are held on the summit of the hill from time to time, during which the priest and congregation circle the summit in a clock-wise direction, following a custom older than their own faith. Linked to the slaying of a mythical beast, the hilltop church is dedicated to St Michael, the dragon slayer. Close by in Brasparts village, a Calvary depicts St Michael slaying a dragon, no doubt a further link with the hill-top chapel.

Alignments and remote standing stones mark other hilltops and moorland crossings, further evidence of the pre-Christian importance of these high moors.

The view to the north-east from Ménez-Mikel overlooks a wide valley now flooded by the reservoir which provides water for a nuclear power station at Brennillis. Before it was flooded, the hollow was an impenetrable peat bog known as the Mouth of Hell, the *Youdig*. A place of ghosts and hob goblins, who terrified the locals until the rector of Brennillis exorcised these tormentors of the living. The fringes of the reservoir are still marshy, providing the perfect environment for bog plants such as insectivorous sundew. A nature trail marked by orange signs follows the banks and swamplands from a car park above the dam at the Brennillis end of the reservoir.

(B) The Alignment. The strange dog-leg of low-lying boulders seems to form a link between Ménez-Mikel and a ridgetop crossroads marked by a menhir further to the east. Possibly some form of communication, their modern counterparts are the telecommunication masts standing on the tops of nearby hills.

Local folklore suggests that the boulders are people turned to stone because they danced on the Sabbath. Ancient stones frequently have stories of dancers turned to stone associated with them, perhaps a folk memory of long-dead pagan festivals. Even nowadays groups of people dance and hold ceremonies around such sites; i.e. the Summer solstice Druidic festival at Stonehenge in Wiltshire.

(C) A little to the south of the road crossing at this point, the *Maison des Artisans* is a craft centre set up by the regional park authority. On display, and also for sale, are many high-quality examples of paintings, sculptures, pottery, and gold and silver work.

(D) Viewpoint. The dramatic and mysteriously rocky cone of Ménez-Mikel rises starkly out of the surrounding moor to the north.

Walk 23
LOCRONAN'S MONTAGNE DU PRIEURÉ 7 km (4 miles) Moderate

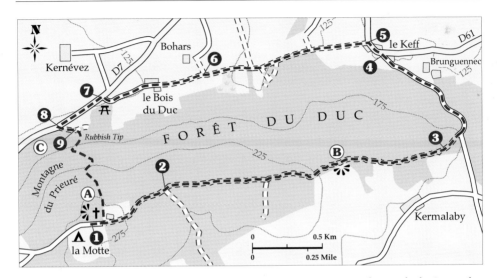

In the fifth century, the Irish saint Ronan built himself a cell on a wooded hilltop, high above what became the town which bears his name; Locronan. Nothing remains of his original cell, but a chapel built on its site, to the east of the town, is a major feature in a *pardon*, or religious procession, around what has since become a holy mountain, the Montagne du Prieuré.

The *pardon*, known locally as a *troménie*, from the Breton *Tro Minihy*, a 'Walk of Retreat', follows a route which has been recorded as far back as the eleventh century. Every sixth year the Grande Troménie circles the mountain, and on each of the other five years, the Petite Troménie climbs the mountain to St Ronan's chapel.

This walk is based on part of the Grande Troménie and begins at St Ronan's chapel. A high level forest track winds its way eastwards from the chapel, through the Forêt du Duc, the Duke's Forest. Side roads and linking farm tracks lead back to the chapel by way of the walk's one and only steep climb.

There is everything from simple snack bars, to crêperies and high-class restaurants in Locronan, catering for all culinary needs, or wallets.

How to get there: Locronan is off the D39 Plonévez-Porzay to Quimper road, which by-passes the traffic-free town. Leave the D39 at the island to the north of the town and follow the D7, Châteaulin road, to the next traffic island. Follow signs for Locronan's car parks off the island, then within a few metres, turn left on to a side road, then quickly right at the next road junction. Follow this road towards the upper car park, but before reaching it make a sharp left-hand turn, past modern houses, then begin to climb steeply up the wooded hill. Ignoring a side road to the left of a small traffic island, continue up the hill. Bear left at the next road junction and drive on towards the chapel which will be on your left at the end of the surfaced road. There is no official car park, but use the verge at the side of the road.

Route description

❶ Walk forwards, slightly uphill, with the chapel on your left, past a modern house and across small meadows in wood-

land clearings. Begin to go gently downhill along a wide sandy track and into dense natural woodland.

❷ Ignoring any side paths on

your right, continue to follow the forest track, steadily downhill all the time.

❸ Continue down a wide forest drive to join a woodland road

next to a sign banning the picking of mushrooms. Turn left on to the road and follow a sweeping left-hand bend, downhill beneath the dappled shade of the branches of trees overhanging the road.

4 Bear left at the road junction beside a group of houses and walk on for another 150m (164yds) to a track junction which is on your left beyond an attractive cottage.

5 Turn left, away from the road, and follow the track, alongside a couple of fields, then to the right of a woodland boundary. Walk forwards, ignoring side tracks right and left, and go past a series of narrow fields and strips of woodland.

6 Continue ahead at the track junction which leads to a group of farm buildings on your right. Still following the field track, go past a nursery garden and a group of scattered cottages and a farmhouse. The track is surfaced from the houses, use it to reach the main road.

7 Join the main road beside a picnic site and turn left. Follow the road for about 300m (328yds), past an open field on your left.

8 Leave the road and turn left on to a track beside the forest boundary. Walk up the track as far as the entrance to a rubbish tip.

9 Turn right beside the tip's boundary fence and follow the woodland path which zig-zags steeply uphill through deciduous forest. As the gradient eases, the path widens and follows the edge of a clearing which leads to the hilltop road and St Ronan's chapel.

Points of interest

Ⓐ Viewpoint, St Ronan's Chapel. The simple woodland chapel is built on the site of St Ronan's cell and is an important halt on the the Grande Troménie de Locronan which takes place every sixth year on the second and third Sundays in July.

The medieval town of Locronan is below, and a little to your right, when facing downhill. Beyond the town, the undulating countryside leads on towards the huge sweep of the Baie de Douarnenez. An old legend speaks of the beautiful island city of Is buried beneath its waves. The city of Is was the home of King Gradlon who ruled Brittany in the sixth century. It was protected from the sea at high tide by gates opened by a key which never left the king's possession. Unfortunately, his beautiful daughter, Dahut, fell in love with a handsome young man who was in fact the Devil in disguise. Jealous of the beauty of Is, the Devil plotted its destruction, and he did it by tricking Dahut into stealing her father's keys. When the Devil opened the gates and flooded the island, King Gradlon led his people on to the mainland where they built what became the city of Quimper. Everyone did not live happily ever after, because during the retreat from the island, Dahut was thrown off her father's horse and fell into the sea. Here she became a mermaid, eventually making a fresh career for herself by luring sailors to their untimely deaths.

Ⓑ Viewpoint. Looking south from the forest the view is of the south Finistère countryside leading to the medieval town of Quimper (pronounced Kimper).

Ⓒ Locronan is ahead and as the signpost claims, the 15-17thC city of character is one of the most beautiful towns in France.

The town once provided sailcloth for the French navy, but as the need for it declined, Locronan simply sat back and let time go by, rather than diversify into other industries. As a result, we are left with one of the most picturesque town centres in Brittany. Granite houses, both elegant and quaint, lean crazily over the narrow alleys and streets leading out from the cobbled central square.

The church is dedicated to St Ronan and has an interestingly decorated pulpit and some fine stained glass in its windows. The belfry tower provides a rooftop view of the town and surrounding farmland, and is open to the public. The fourteenth century chapel of Notre-Dame-de-Bonne-Nouvelle is down a nearby side street; in another, the Maison des Artisans houses displays of local crafts. There are also demonstrations of glass-blowing at the Verriere du Ponant on the Châteaulin road, and the Atelier St Ronan specialises in high quality fabrics.

Locronan's two-storied museum has a section devoted to the history of the area's *pardons*, as well as a display of local costumes and pottery.

Walk 24
POULLAN-SUR-MER   12 km (7.5 miles)   Easy/Moderate

Whoever gave Poullan-sur-Mer its name was perhaps being a little over optimistic. The sea is a good two kilometres (1¼ miles) away, but at least the village is joined to the coast by a network of rural lanes and trackways, and it is a handful of these that are used on this walk.

Quiet by-ways wander between lush fields and link scattered farmsteads and sleepy hamlets to the parent village. Poullan is the market place, the headquarters of the local football club, the hub of social activity and shopping centre for the surrounding countryside. There is also a popular and well-appointed camp site just outside the village, and this walk is an ideal way for anyone staying there to explore the local countryside and coastline.

The village does not have any particularly top grade restaurants, but the bar/cafés and crâperies are mostly family-run and offer excellent value for money. There are also several food shops if you want to make a picnic. The grassy ledge above Porz Meilh, overlooking the sea about half way round the walk, makes an ideal stopping place for a picnic.

How to get there: Poullan-sur-Mer is on the D7 coastal road between Douarnenez and the Pointe du Van, about seven kilometres (four miles) west of Douarnenez. Limited parking is available in the market square in front of the church, or in side streets.

Route description

1 From the square, go to the right of the church, past the chemist's shop and follow the minor road away from the main road, as far as a crossroads with two side lanes.

2 At the crossroads, turn right along the side lane, past two or three houses, then go to the left at a fork. Follow this side road to the outskirts of the village. Go over another crossroads, then out between open fields along a kilometre-long dog-legging lane.

3 Bear right, then left, over the staggered crossroads. Go past the side turning and a line of trees on the left and continue along the surfaced lane, gently downhill to reach the group of farmsteads and cottages at Kerandraon.

4 Take the second turning on the right in Kerandraon and follow the farm lane, between commercial greenhouses, and make towards a small wood. Turn right at a T-junction, then left through the wood, steeply downhill to reach the coast. Turn left and follow the clifftop path.

5 Go past a side path on the left and continue along the cliff path, round the headland of Pointe de la Jument. Keep to the winding path around the tops of coves and little bays.

6 Scramble through a jumble of rocks tumbling down the steep slopes leading to the clifftop.

N.B. Take care when climbing through the boulder field; the rocks can be slippery, especially after rain.

7 Go downhill into a narrow side valley flowing down to the sea. Keep to the seaward i.e. to the right, of a group of trees sheltering the house high on your left.

8 Cross the stream in the valley bottom by hopping over convenient boulders. Climb the hillside above the stream by using the wooden steps to the right in order to reach the cliff edge again.

9 Go beyond a side path to continue along the top of the high cliff. Follow the path around the tops of steep gullies leading down to rocky coves and around small blunted headlands.

10 Turn left on a path leading away from the coast to reach an access drive. Follow the drive beside fields and above a shallow wooded side valley, climbing out towards the upper sheltered fields.

11 Turn left at a T-junction and follow the surfaced road, across the top of the side valley and climb the slope up to the small hamlet of Pennarun.

12 Ignore a side lane to the left on entering Pennarun. Walk towards the main group of houses and, where the road divides, take the left fork. Follow the dog-leg of the lane, between fields, and head gently uphill to the next group of houses.

13 Turn right at the junction with a lane leading into the straggling hamlet of Livroac'h on your left. Follow the tree-lined road, uphill to another T-junction.

14 Left at the T-junction and follow the side road downhill for about 120 metres (131yds), then take the farm track on the right. Follow it for a little over 270 metres (295yds), past side turnings, and follow the track around a sharp left-hand bend. Go forwards between fields for another 200 metres (218yds), past a side track on the right, then walk on between fields for another 350 metres (383yds), and join a road.

15 Turn right on joining the road and head towards the football stadium near houses marking the outskirts of Poullan.

16 Continue to follow the road, over the small square created by the junction with two side roads, and enter Poullan beside its church.

Points of interest

A Viewpoint from Pointe de la Jument across the Baie de Douarnenez and looking towards the Crozon peninsula, the nearest point of which is the coastguard station on top of the limestone cliffs of the Cap de la Chèvre. Coastal shipping passing this spot will be heading in or out of Douarnenez, to the east further along the coast.

B Viewpoint into the rocky inlet of Porz Meilh, a typical open cove on this part of the Brittany coast. The clifftop path is part of the ancient coastguard's patrol route, dating from Napoleonic times.

C Viewpoint. Sea birds feed from the rich inshore waters, beyond the rocky coast. Cormorants are fairly common; they are black with narrow wings and fly low over the sea, or sit deep in the water. Expert underwater hunters, they literally fly beneath the sea in search of their prey. Drying themselves afterwards is a problem and they can be seen hunched on isolated rocks with wings spread to catch the wind.

D The upright splinter of rock on the grassy knoll beside the path and immediately above the side valley, looks suspiciously like a menhir, but it is not shown as such on any map.

E Viewpoint. Looking westwards along the coast to Pointe du Milier and its lighthouse which acts as a guide for shipping along this treacherous coast.

Walk 25
POINTE DU RAZ
                                          7 km (4 miles)   Easy/Moderate

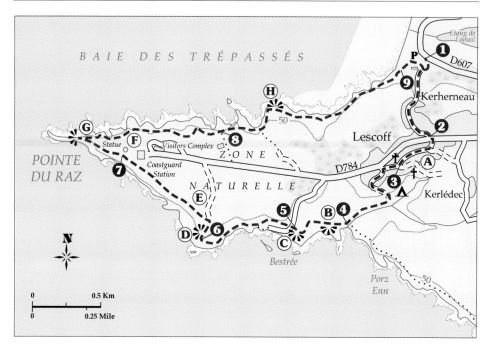

The Pointe du Raz, which is the western tip of the Sizun peninsula and the southern limits of the Baie de Douarnenez, is the subject of this breezy stroll. Visited by over a million people each year along with its neighbour across the Baie des Trépassés, the Pointe du Van, the headland still retains its air of wilderness and mystery. The walk is along the clifftops on either side of the cape, avoiding contact with the coachloads of tourists who come to gaze in awe at only a small fraction of the dramatic sea-scape.

Refreshments can be bought at the visitor complex near the road end above the point, but the best menus can be found at both of the hotel/restaurants by the Baie des Trépassés, where the walk begins and ends.

How to get there: The northerly coastal route follows the D7 from Douarnenez to the Pointe du Van, then south along a minor road to the Baie des Trépassés. A southern route follows the D784 west from Quimper, via Plozévet and Audierne (signposted from there to the Pointe du Raz), as far as Kerherneau. Turn right on entering the village, on to the D607 (Pointe du Van road), downhill for about 750 metres (820yds) to the car park beside the Hotel de la Baie des Trépassés.

Route description

1 Climb the winding sandy track away from the beach and to the right of the road. Go to the left of two white cottages and join a surfaced lane climbing steadily past a communal laundry tank, onwards towards the village.

2 Cross the main road diagonally left to go down a side lane on the right. Follow the lane, winding past groups of white-painted stone cottages. Keep to the wider lane and ignore side turnings.

3 Where the lane forks beside a stone cross, take the right-hand road, uphill. Turn left on reaching the next junction, opposite a private garage, and follow a gradually narrowing track downhill towards the sea. Beyond the last houses, the track loses its surface to bear right and becomes a wide grassy path bordered by bracken and gorse.

❹ On reaching a rocky cove, turn right uphill, along the cliff path winding across turf-covered minor headland, high above steep-sided coves and inlets.

❺ Cross the harbour access track and continue ahead along the gravel and turf-surfaced coastal path.

A short diversion left, down to the harbour, is recommended at this point. The cliff path can be rejoined by a side path angling left, uphill away from the harbour.

❻ To avoid a steep and dangerously open section of the coastline, a wider and safer path turns right, away from the headland, and moves inland, uphill for a short distance to reach a track junction. Turn left at the junction, following an almost level path back towards, then along, the top of the rocky cliffs. Keep to the left of the coastguard station on approaching the headland.

❼ Walk forwards past the dramatic statue, to the limits of the Pointe du Raz. Turn right at the point and begin to follow the path along the northern coastline of the point. Follow the rocky coastline well to the left of the restaurants and snack bars of the visitor complex.

❽ Take the left-hand of the paths at the junction below, and a little way beyond, the old white-painted hotel on your right. Use the orange spot waymarks of the *Sentier Côtier*, to keep to the correct route.

❾ Keeping to the left of the two white cottages, slant left downhill along the grassy path heading towards the sand dunes and beach-side car park of the Baie des Trépassés.

Points of interest

Ⓐ Religion plays an important part in the everyday lives of fishermen trawling the waters off this dangerous coast. Lescoff has numerous stone crosses dotted about its side lanes and back alleys. The pretty village church is dedicated to St Michel, giving rise to the theory that it is built on the site of an earlier pagan Celtic religious site.

Ⓑ Viewpoint. The sea has worn its way through a band of softer rock, creating a natural arch below the coastal path at this point.

Ⓒ Viewpoint. A bench seat offers an ideal stopping place to admire the tiny and attractive fishing harbour of Bestrée. Nature provided strategically-placed rocks which only needed joining in order to create a sheltered anchorage against the harsh south-westerly storms.

Ⓓ Viewpoint. The barren ocean-washed cliffs of the Pointe du Raz lead the eye towards the tiny off-shore Île-de-Sein. The finger of the headland's lighthouse acts to guide shipping negotiating the treacherous waters swirling round the dramatic promontory.

Ⓔ The moors and clifftops of the Pointe du Raz have been designated a *Zone Naturelle* in order to protect its special wildlife, and also to repair and control the erosion created by the million visitors each year.

Ⓕ A dramatic statue of Notre Dame des Naufragés looks sadly out over a coast which has been the scene of all too many shipwrecks.

Ⓖ Viewpoint. The dramatic cliffs of the sea-washed headland look out across a wild tidal race towards the Île-de-Sein. The low-lying island, the site of ancient Celtic legend, is the home of fishermen and their wives who tend the tiny wall-sheltered fields. A proud and independent group of people who have rescued countless shipwrecked mariners, their greatest act of bravery took place during World War 2. On 18 June 1940, and in answer to General de Gaulle's call, all 130 men of military age sailed to Britain to join the Free French forces. In 1946, the Île de Sein was visited personally by General de Gaulle in order to award the island the Cross of Liberation.

A birdwatcher's paradise, the Île de Sein can be reached by a ferry from Audierne, further to the east along the Crozon peninsula.

Ⓗ Viewpoint overlooking the Baie des Trépassés. The dune-locked bay is linked to several legends. All are based on its possible derivation from the old Breton title of the *Boe an Anoan*, the Bay of Souls. One version says that in the time of the old Celtic religion, when the local Druidic priests died they were ferried out from the bay for burial on the Île de Sein. There is also a suggestion that King Gradlon's legendary city of Is was not off Douarnenez (see Walk 23), but is lost beneath the waters of this bay. A final, and perhaps more acceptable story surrounding the title, is based on the fact that tidal currents tended to wash drowned sailors into the bay.

To the right of the beach road, the small reedy lake has been created by the natural dam of storm-washed shingle. Many visiting sea birds, especially waders, make their nests along its grassy shore.

Walk 26
PORZ POULHAN

8 km (5 miles)   Easy

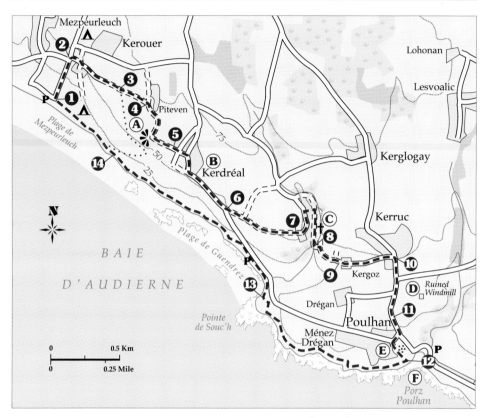

Tiny farms amidst early cropping fields, a Celtic missionary's chapel, the ruins of an old mill and a colourful fishing harbour overlooked by the enigmatic group of stones of long forgotten Druidic ceremonies, are linked by a coastal path skirting tiny rocky coves and sandy beaches. Acting as an ever-present backcloth to this pleasant ramble is the azure sea with its constantly changing views.

The friendly stone-built harbourside bar/restaurant at Porz Poulhan conveniently marks the half-way point, and there is also a crêperie next to the car park above the beach of Plage de Mezpeurleuch, at the end of the walk.

How to get there: D784 west from Quimper (Audierne road), via Plozévet to Plouhinec. Take the first road on the left past the centre of Plouhinec and go down to the Plage de Mezpeurleuch (signposted). Car park next to the beach.

Route description

❶ From the car park walk back uphill along the Plouhinec road, almost to the top of the first rise.

❷ Take the first road turning on the right, along a side lane lead-ing to a group of cottages. Go over the first crosstracks and head forwards along a grassy track between tiny stone-walled fields and to your right of a market garden.

❸ Ahead at the fork, following the more prominent track leading towards a line of pine trees and cottages on the skyline.

❹ Bear right at the track junc-tion and keep to the seaward side of the cottages. Follow a track winding between a series of un-walled cultivated fields. Head beyond the fields towards a small village.

⑤ Join a surfaced lane and follow it, over crossroads, then bear right along the lane curving through the village. Bear left where the lane is joined by a minor track from the right.

⑥ Turn left beside a signpost indicating *Sentier PR 10*, along an unsurfaced track, climbing gently uphill. Ignore side turnings and follow the track beside a line of telegraph posts, at first beside tiny fields on your left, then with gorse and rough moorland on either side.

⑦ Go past a farm cottage and turn left to follow its access drive for about 130 metres (142yds). Where the drive begins to veer left, turn sharp right and go down a narrow path between dense gorse and broom bushes to join a cart track. Turn right along the track, heading towards a tiny chapel. Go past the chapel, down-hill along a grassy path swinging left into the valley bottom.

⑧ Cross the stream by a concrete slab bridge and begin to climb, gradually right, past a laundry well, uphill on a steadily widening path. Keep to the right at a couple of track junctions and go towards a group of farm buildings.

⑨ Go through the farmyard and out along the access drive, aiming towards a clump of roadside trees.

⑩ Turn right when you reach the road and walk downhill towards the coast. Ignoring side turnings, walk on towards the village.

⑪ On entering the village, bear right at the road junction, then left, following the signpost point-ing to the *Allée Couverte*. After vis-iting the stones, take the grassy path down to the harbour.

⑫ Follow a stony track around the rocky coastline to the right and away from the harbour. Go past the harbour light and take the path to the left of cottage number 18. Walk on, skirting rocky coves and tiny sandy beaches along the low coastline.

⑬ Where the path disappears on reaching a wide sandy beach, go towards, but not quite up to, the road on your right, then bear left, through the beach car park beside the Plage de Guendrez. Walk through low sand dunes above the beach to rejoin the well-defined sandy coastal path on the far side of the beach.

⑭ When you reach sand dunes bordering the beach at the Plage de Mezperleuch, keep to the right and go through them, but do not cross the camp site boundary. Walk on towards the car park.

Points of interest

Ⓐ Viewpoint looking west over the fields and scattered cottages to the picturesque fishing port of Audierne at the mouth of the River Goyen. There is a lobster and crab farm at Audierne which is open to visitors, and also a

thatched cottage museum dating from the seventeenth century called *la Chaumière*, which is furnished with antique Breton furniture and kitchen utensils.

Ⓑ The hamlet of Kerdréal on your left is worth a diversion to admire the grouping of sturdy south Finistère cottages and their pretty gardens.

Ⓒ The tiny chapel, almost hidden in the valley bottom, is dedicated to St They, an early Celtic missionary.

Ⓓ A stunted tower on a low hillock, to the left of the road as you enter Poulhan, is all that is left of a windmill where the local people once ground their flour.

Ⓔ *Allée Couverte*. An enigmatic double row of tall grey stones topped by massive slabs, and sur-rounded by an irregular outer oval of smaller rocks, stands in a small field between houses over-looking the harbour at Poulhan. A signpost points the way from lower streets, and a plaque explains the history of this strange collection of stones which date from around 3300-2800 B.C. Its use, like all the other ancient stone structures throughout Brittany, is open to conjecture, but the fact that the *allée* appears to be roofed, leads to the theory that it was some form of Druidic temple.

Ⓕ The tiny harbour at Porz Poulhan, filled with colourful fishing boats of all types and backed by a convenient bar/restaurant, is made for exploring.

Walk 27
CIRCUIT DE ST KODELIG

9 km (6 miles)   Easy

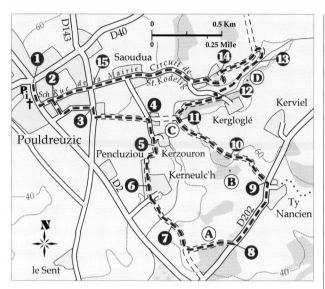

The *Circuit de St Kodelig* follows a winding route of field tracks and woodland paths around the little rural town of Pouldreuzic. The walk, one of several 'circuits' in the area (you can find details of the others at Pouldreuzic's Information Centre) passes three menhirs (standing stones) associated with the early Celtic saint in whose honour this walk is named. Pouldreuzic can hardly be said to be on any tourist trail, but even so it has several interesting nooks and crannies worth investigating. The walk also offers a useful excuse for a break during a long drive north or south through Brittany. There is a small zoo specialising in European fauna off the D2 just a little under 2.5 kilometres (1½ miles) south-east of the town.

Pont l'Abbé is the nearest town of note. As the name suggests, the town is built around a bridge erected by the monks who lived at the nearby ancient monastery of Loctudy. The bridge crosses one of the complex of marshy inlets of the Anse du Pouldon, a river estuary famous for its oyster farms. The skills of Breton embroidery are kept very much alive here, with the famous stove-pipe hats, *coiffes*, being worn by the ladies of the town on every special occasion, especially at the *Fête des Brodeuses*, the Embroidery Fair, which is held on the second Sunday in July. The Musée Bigouden, in the ancient fourteenth-century castle keep, houses a collection of dolls in traditional costume, and traces the development of the Breton stovepipe hats. It also has a fine collection of model ships.

An old farm which is open to visitors, the Maison du Pays Bigouden, about 2 km (1 mile) along the Loctudy road from Pont l'Abbé, has been restored in the traditional style of the district.

Pouldreuzic cannot boast any restaurants of note, but it has the usual bars and a handful of food shops.

How to get there: Pouldreuzic is on the D2 road between Pont l'Abbé and Plozévet, to the west of Quimper. Park next to the community centre, which also doubles as the local tourist information office.

Route description
❶ Turn right away from the tourist office and walk along the main street, past the church and turn left along the Rue de la Mairie.
❷ Turn right opposite the junior school and walk down the narrow street. Go to the left at a T-junction marked by a line of trees. Follow the minor road onwards past modern houses and up to a busier road.
❸ Go to the right at a T-junction, cross over to a hardware store set back from the road. Go past the shop and turn left to follow a grassy field track beside its boundary hedge. Aim towards the cottage at the end of the track.
❹ Turn right along the lane, but where it turns left towards a group of houses, continue ahead on an unsurfaced field track.
❺ Go to the right, then left, along the track, through double right-angled bends and then between intensive rearing sheds.
❻ Go past the farmhouse and turn right at the lane junction, then immediately left along a sunken track beneath the shade of overhanging trees.
❼ Where the track climbs out of a damp hollow, continue ahead at the track junction, between gorse bushes on your left and an open field to the right. Go forwards,

then bear left and go under a power line, and pass between grassed-over WW2 concrete gun emplacements. Bear slightly to the right, through rough scrub to reach a surfaced road.

8 At the road turn left and follow it steadily uphill for 600 metres (656yds), towards a group of houses and farm buildings.

9 Turn left opposite a bungalow and walk along a cart track heading towards, then into mixed woodland.

10 Inside the woods, and on reaching the interpretive plaque, turn half right and follow yellow waymarks downhill through the woods.

11 Where the track reaches a stream, do not cross the stone clapper bridge on your left, but go a little to the right, slightly uphill along the grassy track. Follow it beside a narrow stream until it reaches a road.

12 Turn left at the road and cross the stream, then go forwards to a bench seat. Turn right at the seat, along a wide grassy woodland path.

13 Follow the path, climbing sharply to the left and widening to a track, out of the woodland glade. Keeping to the path, follow it beside a couple of fields and continue ahead where it forms a junction with a field track. Head towards a cluster of buildings at the far end of the next field.

14 Turn left at the farm, following the track around it and its small orchard, then go to the right as you reach some cottages. Follow the surfaced lane and go with it to the left at a junction beyond the orchard. Continue along the rural lane, winding across a wide shallow valley.

15 Follow the lane over a wider road and go past modern houses; then gradually past older properties until you reach the junior school. Continue along the street, then turn right at the main road. Go past the church to reach the car park.

Points of interest

A The massive concrete structures are World War 2 gun emplacements, part of the second line of defence behind Hitler's Atlantic Wall. They were part of the complex system created to defend the Atlantic ports of Brest and St Nazaire and their U-Boat bases. Fortunately, the guns housed in these emplacements were overrun without a shot being fired, and so the wartime relics now slowly moulder into insignificance.

B St Kodelig's Menhir. The saint preached his Christian message next to this stone. The stone, and others throughout the wood associated with the saint, have been endowed with magical properties, handed down across the centuries. Several have been given fanciful names, such as St Kodelig's Bed. A small plaque next to the menhir tells the story in English.

The Story of St Kodelig

Once upon a time a very charitable old man is said to have lived here at the top of the hill.

He left some pieces of furniture like the wardrobe (a huge high stone), a pat of butter, a stele (a marked stone) and his bed (the lying stone).

Several of the trees in the woods surrounding the menhir were killed by a fire several years ago.

C A stone clapper bridge, over the little woodland stream beside the ford on the left of the track, suggests that the pathways have been in use since the Middle Ages, if not since pre-historic times. Then they would have seen a greater use, but now it is only the occasional farmer on his tractor or walker who passes by.

D The large stone on the right, the Menhir de Morvé, is also known as St Kodelig's wardrobe.

Walk 28
THE ALIGNMENTS OF CARNAC

6 km (4 miles)   Easy

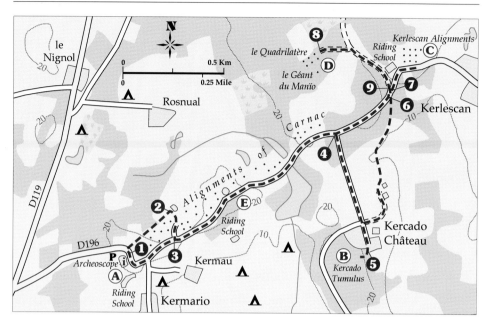

Megaliths, dolmens, allées couvertes, tumuli and other standing stones, dot the coastline and inland fields of Brittany. No matter how many of these strange remains one finds while exploring this ancient land, to turn the corner of a side road and find the first of Carnac's alignments always comes as a shock. Lines of thousands of low grey stones march into the distance. To anyone acquainted with the massive bulk of Stonehenge, the stones of Carnac might at first glance be smaller than expected. However, what they lack in height is more than compensated for by an emanation of calm, yet imposing, presence.

Built in the middle of the Neolithic period around 4,000 to 3,000 B.C., over 3,000 follow a rough northeast, south-westerly swathe to the north of Carnac. Arranged in four groups together with satellite tumuli and independent standing stones, they form an impressive memorial to a long dead civilisation.

Carnac is the world's premier site for megalithic monuments. Various astronomical theories surround the alignments, but none have been proven satisfactorily. A visiting American officer at the end of World War 2 even thought they were German tank traps! An older legend says that they are the legionaries of a Roman army which God turned to stone to stop them harrying the early Christian Saint Cornély.

The first group nearest to Carnac is the Ménec system and are usually the first to be seen on approaching the alignment complex from the main road. As one turns the bend, the road skirts the nearest of eleven lines of roughly parallel stones, partly hidden behind clumps of maritime pines. Starting from a circle of stones in the back gardens and courtyards of the village of le Ménec, the alignments march beside the road for 1200 metres (1313yds). Beyond them is the major group, the Kermario alignments. Gradually diminshing in height from 6.40 to 0.50 metres (21 to 1½ feet), the stones draw the eye towards a low hill, the distance apparently increased by the artificially created perspective of the diminishing sizes. Not quite parallel, the alignments have extra features such as an allée couverte and other smaller 'sanctuaries'.

On the brow of the low-wooded hill beyond the Kermario alignment, two dramatic structures, the huge Manïo menhir and the hollow tumulus at Kercado, precede the thirteen rows of alignments which fan out from a rectangular enclosure at Kerlescan. Finally, the smaller groups of Petit Ménec are built as incomplete semi-circles and gently inward-curving lines.

The Festival of Menhirs, when the alignments are blessed by the local clergy, takes place on the third Sunday in August.

Carnac's church is dedicated to St Cornély, the patron saint of farm animals. A mural depicting him surrounded by oxen and other farm animals, stands above the church's main entrance door.

The walk described here is, by necessity, partly by road, and also returns by some of the outward route, but this is a small price to pay to experience the magical wonder of the Alignments of Carnac. A tour of the ancient stone monuments can be improved by visiting the *Musée Préhistoire* in Carnac where many of the artefacts found during archaeological investigations in the region are displayed.

There is usually a small caravan snack-bar parked by the visitor centre at the start of the Kermario alignments, but the crêperie beside the tumulus near Kercado Château is more comfortable and is at roughly the half-way point. The nearest restaurants can be found near the camp sites to the north of the alignments, or in Carnac itself.

How to get there: D781 to traffic lights in the northern outskirts of Carnac. Follow the D196, signposted to the 'Alignments', past the village of le Ménec and park at the *Accueil*, Information and Visitor Centre.

Route description

1 After visiting the information centre, the *Archeoscope*, follow the fence along the left-hand side (as facing) of the alignments until you reach a farmhouse.

2 Turn right at the farm, along its access lane across the middle of the stone rows. Go past a group of four massive stones at the roadside.

3 Turn left and follow the road, but keep to the verge and avoid oncoming traffic while admiring the alignments. Follow the road over the headwaters of an attractive, tree-shaded reservoir.

4 Turn right and walk down the avenue towards Kercado Château. Go to the right following signs for the crêperie and the tumulus.

5 From the crêperie go back towards the château. Cross the head of the driveway and follow the cart track on the right past two adjacent restored stone cottages. Continue by footpath into woodland, then bear right and walk towards the road.

6 Turn right and follow the tree-lined road, beyond the riding school in order to visit the Kerlescan Alignments. Return to the riding school.

7 Immediately next to the riding school a narrow woodland track turns right. Follow it in and out of the tree-shade, between two fields, and where the track forks, go to the left and towards a clearing dominated by the massive *Géant du Manïo* menhir and the *Quadrilatère*.

8 Return through the forest to reach the road again.

9 Turn right to follow the road back beside the alignments and over the reservoir, all the way back to the car park.

Points of interest

A Allow plenty of time (at least 2½ hours) for the walk and use a good portion of it studying the excellent model of the alignments and other items on display inside the information centre. The ideal way to view the alignments is from the air. The next best alternative is to use the viewing platform outside the visitor centre to pick out the features of the lines of stones winding their way into the distance.

B Kercado Tumulus. The huge grassy mound covers a ring of upright stones topped by an apparently unsupported flat boulder. Several of the stones have carvings of daggers and other symbolic features, as old as the structure itself.

C The Kerlescan Alignments. Separated by a low hill from the main alignments, those at Kerlescan have thirteen roughly parallel lines leading from a rectangular enclosure beyond the riding school.

D The solitary menhir known as the *Géant du Manïo* stands like an eerie sentinel in the middle of the woodland clearing. A little to one side, an oblong of low stones called the *Quadrilatère*, looks as though it was meant to be used as a stockade for sacrificial animals, or a plot for growing special herbs.

E Turn off the road and cross the alignments to reach the small stone tower. From its summit there is a view looking back towards the information centre, of the Kermario alignments. Beyond them is a colossal tumulus mound topped by the Church of St Michel. 125 metres (137yds) long, 60 metres (66yds) wide and 10 metres (11yds) high, it dates from around 3,500 B.C. Excavations in 1862 and 1900-1906 revealed numerous beutifully-carved stone objects and jewellery which are now on display in the Carnac Museum.

Walk 29
RIVES DE MERRIEN

5 km (3 miles)   Easy

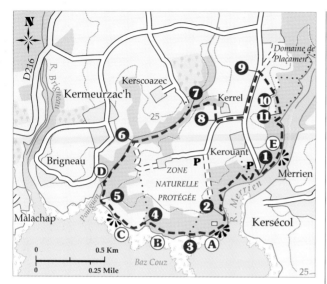

In order to protect the special beauty of the coast, moorland and river banks around the mouth of the River Merrien (the *Rives de Merrien*), this area has been designated a *Zone Naturelle Protégée*. The equivalent in Britain would be a Site of Special Scientific Interest (SSSI).

There are no facilities to hand on this walk, but nearby Moëlan-sur-Mer is only four kilometres (2½ miles) away, and has a good selection of shops, bars and restaurants.

How to get there: N165-E60 to Quimperlé. D16 and D116 to Moëlan. D216 south-west to cross roads at Ty-Poulbraz. Unclassified road south via Plaçamen and Kerouant. (Signposted Presqu'île de Merrien.) Car park at the road end.

Route description

1 Looking towards the river, turn right from the car park and follow the tree-shaded path above the estuary. Walk towards the headland, continuing ahead at the path junction.

2 Go to the right, away from the coast, towards the little fort peeping above the gorse bushes, then go left from it, back down to the coast. Swing right and follow the clifftop path.

3 Keep to the left at the path junction, continuing to follow the coast.

4 Walk round the little cove and bear left at the next path junction.

5 Follow the path around the deeply indented cove at Poulguen. Do not cross the entrant stream, but turn right away from the sea, to follow a footpath into woodland beside a marshy stream.

6 Ahead at the path junction, and continue to walk gently uphill beneath the trees.

7 Turn right at the junction and follow the more prominent woodland path uphill. Go round a sharp right-hand bend and then

left to leave the woods. Cross the meadow to the right of a group of tree-shaded farm buildings and walk towards a minor road.

8 Turn left and walk down the road until it joins another at a T-junction. Turn left to follow this second road between fields for about 340 metres (372yds).

9 Within sight of gates into the park of Domaine de Plaçamen, turn right along a wide tree-lined path heading into woodland.

10 Go to the right at the woodland track junction, downhill then left at a fork. Continue through the forest as far as the river.

11 Turn right on the woodland path, high above the river bank and follow it back to the car park.

Points of interest

A Viewpoint. Looking out over the Bay of Biscay. To your immediate left is the sheltered harbour at the mouth of the River Merrien. The curious stone building on your right is a restored customs post and is worth visiting.

B Rock pools in the cove to your left will reward a spell of beachcombing. Access is by way of the low jumble of rocks on its far side, but keep an eye on the fast incoming tide.

C Viewpoint. Across the wooded cove and beyond the next headland, the little hamlet of Malachap sits attractively above the mouth of the River Brigneau.

D Woodlands surrounding the marshy stream are of special interest to naturalists. Flowers, such as the bright yellow flag iris, bloom well into summer. Shy woodland birds and foxes also use the safety of the wood's dense undergrowth.

E Viewpoint. Privately-owned pleasure craft and colourful inshore fishing boats anchor in the sheltered waters by the mouth of the Merrien.

Walk 30
FORÊT DOM DE CARNOËT

5 km (3 miles)   Easy

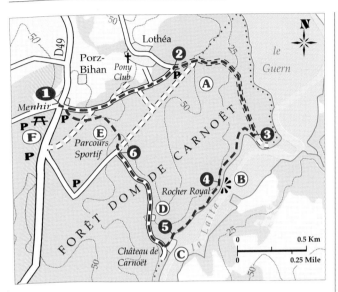

In times gone by, most of the Brittany countryside would have been covered by beech forest, and this riverside stretch is one of the few areas to escape the woodsman's axe.

The walk is along easy forest tracks and can easily be extended along the wide paths and trackways upstream and down.

Specialising in regional dishes, the Restaurant Toulfoën, which is next to the car park at the start of the walk, is highly recommended. Alternatively, there is a very pleasant picnic site in the woodland glade on the opposite side of the road.

How to get there: South from Quimperlé by the D49 le Pouldu road, to a crossroads beside the Restaurant Toulfoën. Car park to the left.

Route description

❶ Follow the quiet forest road, to the right and away from the car park. Ignore any side turnings and go past the entrance to the pony club.

❷ Where the surfaced road turns sharply to the left, go round the traffic barrier on your right and walk down the wide, gravel-surfaced woodland track.

❸ Within sight of the river, go sharp right on to a footpath sign-posted to the *Rocher Royal*. Walk round a swamp and, with the river on your left, walk uphill beneath overhanging beech trees.

❹ Go downhill from the rocky outcrop, still following the woodland path until you reach a secluded château.

❺ Follow the track to the right, around the château and as far as a track junction. Turn sharp right here, uphill along the surfaced forest drive.

❻ Where the surfaced drive turns sharp left at its junction with a track from your right, continue ahead, between the trees and on to a narrow path. Bear right where it joins a Keep Fit Course. Follow the signs for the course in an anti-clockwise direction all the way back to the car park.

Points of interest

Ⓐ In the sixth century, the forest was the domain of the Count de Commorre who lived at the Château de Carnoët (see feature Ⓒ), and who was told by a fortune teller that he would be killed by his son. Five times married, he killed the first four wives when they became pregnant. His fifth, Trepine, escaped into the forest where she gave birth to a son. Angered by this, the count beheaded his wife, but she was restored to life by St Gildas who sewed her head back on. In revenge the saint threw a handful of soil at the château, promptly knocking it down and so killing the count.

Ⓑ Viewpoint. Looking out over the River la Laïta from the Rocher Royal.

Ⓒ The lovely riverside Château de Carnoët stands in one of the most idyllic settings imaginable. Uphill a little way from the château, and almost hidden amongst the trees, are the scant ruins of a Dominican monastery, founded in 1254 by Blanche de Naverre.

Ⓓ The water-fed building on the right of the road is used for breeding trout which are later put into the river.

Ⓔ *Parcours Sportif* – Keep Fit Course. For anyone with energy to spare after the walk.

Ⓕ Behind the picnic site, the menhir, a monolith of gigantic proportions, poses the question: How was it brought here, by whom and for what purpose?

BARTHOLOMEW WALK GUIDES

Bartholomew also publishes **Walking in the Dordogne**, plus an extensive range of Walk Guides covering Britain's best walking country.

Titles in the series include:

Walk the Cornish Coastal Path
Walk the Dales
Walk Dorset & Thomas Hardy's Wessex
Walk Exmoor & the Quantocks
Walk Kent
Walk the Lakes
Walk Loch Lomond & the Trossachs
Walk Loch Ness & the Spey Valley
Walk the New Forest
Walk the North Downs
Walk Northumbria
Walk the North York Moors
Walk Oban, Mull & Lochaber
Walk the Peak District
Walk Perthshire
Walk Skye & Wester Ross
Walk Snowdonia & North Wales
Walk South Devon Coastal Path & Dartmoor
Walk the South Downs
Walk South Wales & the Wye Valley
Walk Surrey

All titles are available from good bookshops,
or telephone HarperCollins Distribution Services
on 0141-772 3200.